Legends
OF LIBERTY

TIMELESS STORIES OF COURAGEOUS CHAMPIONS

COMPILED BY RICK GREEN

Revolutionary Strategies
P.O. Box 900
Dripping Springs, TX 78620
(512) 858-0974
www.RickGreen.com

Cover design: Joshua Russell

Printed in the United States of America
ISBN 9780988352780

INTRODUCTION

BY RICK GREEN

Legend
\'le-jənd

1. a story coming down from the past; especially one popularly regarded as historical although not verifiable;

2. a famous or important person who is known for doing something extremely well;

Liberty
\'li-bər-tē

1. the quality or state of being free; the positive enjoyment of various social, political, or economic rights and privileges;

2. an action going beyond normal limits; risk, chance; deviation from standard practice;

3. ye have been called unto liberty (Galatians 5:13); where the Spirit of the Lord is, there is liberty (2 Corinthians 3:17); Stand fast therefore in the liberty wherewith Christ has made us free (Galatians 5:1);

WHAT or WHO Is A Legend Of Liberty?

All of the stories you about to experience (if we accomplish our goal, it will be more than just reading the story, we want you to experience it) fit somehow, someway into one or all of the common definitions above.

Some of our chosen subjects are well known and their story well documented. Others are only partially documented, with many pieces of the story passed down through history without full documentation or multiple eye witness accounts.

Every subject in this book went way beyond normal limits or typical practice, often at great personal risk or peril, in order to secure liberty for others. Many physically fought, some paying the ultimate price in battle. Others fought with their words and service, helping many to find true liberty in Christ.

Six of our chosen legends are from the American Revolution and two more were instrumental in making America possible, while one legend is from 3,000 years ago. Two played professional baseball in the 20th Century, but they make the cut for our book because of their greater impact on society and world history. Three of our subjects are still living legends and they continue to fight for liberty for others.

WHO Is Telling the Legend?

Fifteen stories are voiced by twelve different people, all with very different writing styles, story-telling techniques, and unique gifts for bringing the legend to life and sharing lessons applicable to all liberty lovers.

We range in age from teenagers to senior citizens. We are professional speakers, comedians, pastors, soldiers, athletes, and students. We very much love our nation. To be a bit cliché, but absolutely sincere, we know that freedom is not free and we want to honor those who answered the call of duty to birth or defend the freedom we now enjoy.

HOW Will The Legend Be Told?

Each chapter will begin with a short introduction of the author, followed by the legend told in the style chosen by the author. Each chapter is different. Some authors contributed more "scholarly" works with well-documented footnotes. Others share heart-felt, personal experiences with a legend they knew well.

Several legends are told in the increasingly popular "faction" or "historical fiction" style. Documented facts of the story are used as benchmarks and parameters. Where little is known of certain details, the author inserts creative writing of what probably happened, or could have happened; while care is taken to make sure the author does not contradict known facts. We do not present these particular chapters as historical fact, but rather as creative, fictional accounts based upon historical fact. When reading these particular chapters, approach them like watching a movie about a historical person or event. Rather than getting caught up in the nuance of the clothing or other things being perfectly correct for the period, stay focused on the theme and life lesson that can be learned.

Some will criticize this blending of fact and fiction and they will scour these pages looking for the opportunity to distract from our purpose by making a mountain out of a mole hill.

We believe the unique story-telling found in these pages is an effective tool for engaging a culture that is increasingly uninterested in history. We are losing the wisdom of the ages because of our self-absorbed arrogance and frenzied schedules.

Our goal with this particular book is not to offer a history book for the classroom. Rather, we wish to provide a collection of inspirational stories that will arouse interest in history and heroes, while provoking citizens of today to become legends of liberty tomorrow.

We are willing to accept the criticism of those who relish the mole hill, as long as this whole process helps you discover the mountains of positive, culture supporting, life-enhancing encouragement found in these pages.

Bringing History to Life...

In many of these chapters, you will join us in the Green Family time machine as you personally witness legends of liberty by stepping back into the moment the events occurred.

When I say "time machine," feel free to picture Marty & Doc's DeLorean (*Back to the Future*), H.G. Wells' Time Sled (*The Time Machine*), or even Bill & Ted's phone booth (*Bill and Ted's Excellent Adventure*). Sorry Potter fans, but Harry's Time-Turner is of no use, because five hours back will not even scratch the surface of where we need to be. Lastly, you might want to avoid the Terminator version of time travel because it looks pretty painful and leaves you looking for new clothes wherever you end up.

Regardless of what you envision for our method of time travel, the important thing is where we are going and the legends of liberty we will witness while there.

So, buckle up, batten down the hatches, and take whatever precautions necessary for your chosen time machine.

First stop... September 11th... New York City... and she is under serious attack when we arrive.

But it's not the 9/11 you're thinking of...

LEGEND 1

NATHAN HALE

VOICED BY:

RICK GREEN

Our time machine arrives on September 11th in New York City and she is under attack.

But if you calibrated the time machine for 2001, you should skip over to Legends #9 or #14. To get a glimpse of this first legend of liberty, we must go WAY back... more than two centuries ago, back to 1776.

The Declaration of Independence has birthed the United States of America barely two months earlier, and there is no turning back for the colonists.

General George Washington freed Boston in March and is slowly turning his army into a genuine fighting force.

All eyes are now on New York City. The British first invaded Statin Island, then defeated the Americans on Long Island, forcing Washington's retreat to Manhattan. The Colonial General is now planning a counter-attack to keep from losing all of New York City.

As both sides dig in, Washington knows he will lose New York unless he can obtain good intelligence on the troop movements and fortifications of the British.

There is only one way to get that information... General Washington needs a spy!

For us living in the Twenty-First Century, the word spy immediately conjures up images of the Hollywood version of a secret agent. You can see him in your mind right now. The fearless, smooth talking, well dressed super-soldier, with all the best gadgets, is able to complete the most impossible of missions, no matter the odds against him. And even when he has no gadgets, he can still kill you with a magazine, toothpick, paperclip or whatever is handy... all while never loosing his composure and ordering that martini "shaken, not stirred."

But the challenge facing George Washington is long before the days of James Bond, Mitch Rapp, Jason Bourne, and Mission Impossible.

In 1776, there is no CIA, no MI6, no Mossad... certainly no loyal American intelligence network at all. In 1776, spies are the lowest of the low, not military heroes. They are hired guns, unsavory and untrustworthy.

Spies are killed upon capture and respected by none.

Washington knows the information he needs cannot be trusted to that type of man. He needs one of his trusted officers for this particular task. But he could not, would not, demand such a dangerous and demeaning mission of anyone... he wants someone to volunteer.

Late at night, Col. Tom Knowlton quietly gathers his officers in a tent at a secret location away from prying eyes and ears. In hushed tones, he asks for a volunteer to answer the General's call.

His request is met with dead silence.

Finally, an older, gruff officer breaks the silence and says, "I am willing to be shot in battle, but I am not willing to be hanged like a dog." In other words, there is no honor in this mission.

Knowlton tries further to persuade and eventually gives up. As he is turning to leave and tell the General he has failed, a young man standing in the doorway of the tent steps forward and simply says with a steady voice, "I will undertake the mission." He has arrived to the meeting late, ill with a fever, but eager to serve.

To fully comprehend the scene before us, you must also know that this secret meeting in the tent is no ordinary group of officers.

The young man at the door is not just any soldier.

These men are an elite special-forces group that Washington has recently formed... they are literally the very first American Rangers.

If it helps, picture Chuck Norris... but with a pony tail!

The courageous volunteer at the door is none other than Nathan Hale. Captain Hale is only 21 years of age, well educated, and by all accounts of the ladies, a handsome fellow to boot!

At the top of his Yale graduating class at the age of 18, Hale is a seriously devoted Christian, planning to become a minister of the gospel. Fresh out of college, he was serving as a teacher when the war broke out.

A well accomplished speaker and debater in college, he argued that the higher education of women was being neglected. So, in addition to serving as the teacher of the Union Grammar School in New London, Conn, he had been teaching a group of ladies from five to seven each morning.

After a year of teaching, "the shot heard round the world" was fired at Lexington, Massachusetts on April 19, 1775. Hale, still in his teens but enrolled in the local militia, attended the town meeting in New London and stood to speak.

"Let us march immediately," he had said, "and never lay down our arms until we obtain independence!" The word "independence" had not yet been spoken of publicly in his town, but the courage of this young man shook the community from the slumber of colonial submission. He then shook the hand of each of his students, prayed with them, and left for war.

Now he finds himself volunteered for the most dangerous and most degrading mission he could imagine.

Standing outside Col. Knowlton's tent, under cover of darkness, Captain Hale's good friend from college, Captain William Hull, tries to change his mind. Hull stresses the dangers of the mission, the likelihood of death, and the dishonorable legacy of being a spy.

Nathan is unmoved and responds by pointing out there is honor in a mission that was so necessary for the cause... his General and his nation need him, and he will do what duty demands!

Hale makes his way behind enemy lines and with his Yale diploma in hand, poses as a teacher looking for a new job. Over the course of several days, he is able to map out the British troop locations and fortifications. With this extremely valuable information hidden in the soul of his shoe, he is captured before he can make his way back across enemy lines.

The evidence is right there on his person.

There is no denying what he is there to do.

He is sentenced to hang the next morning.

Unable to sleep, as he is contemplating his fate, he begins to come to grip with the fact that he has failed. He has failed his mission, his general, and the cause. Hale requests a member of the clergy, but is refused.

He requests a Bible and is refused.

He is finally given paper and pen to write final words to his family. As he calmly pens a letter to his family, he purposes within his heart to do the only thing he could still do to help the cause for which he is willing to die.

The next morning, as people gather to watch the hanging, he is given a chance for last words. Summoning his best oratory and quoting heavily from Joseph Addison's Cato, Captain Nathan Hale gives a passionate defense of the American cause of freedom. British soldiers begin heckling and mocking him for dying for what they say is a worthless and hopeless cause.

He closes with those immortal and inspiring words, "I only regret that I have but one life to give for my country."[1]

Hale's composure, passion, determination, and oratory change his fate and greatly influence the very concept of patriotism.

As women in the crowd weep aloud and even hardened enemy soldiers are moved by his words, the image of a disgraced traitor is transformed into an honorable patriot sacrificing for a worthy cause.

Nearly two and a half centuries later, we can now see the tremendous success of what Nathan Hale believed was a failed mission.

In giving his life, he inspired hope for the cause, stirred conviction and belief in what the Americans were fighting for, and he accomplished a far greater purpose than the recon maps for which he had left camp.

Even today, Hale reminds us that we each have but one life to give.

Every day we give our lives for *something*.

For what will you give *your* one life?

For what will you invest your life today? Or over the next year, or decade?

One of the amazing things about American Exceptionalism is that every generation of Americans, from Nathan Hale in our first generation to heroes like Navy Seal Michael Murphy in this current generation, every generation has had patriots willing to stand up and say, "freedom will not be lost on my watch...even if I must give my one life for the cause of liberty."

Many, just like Nathan Hale, gave their one life for you and for me. They sacrificed so that we might live in freedom, so that we might be free to choose our career, choose our spouse, raise our children as we see fit, worship according to the dictates of our conscience. We enjoy all of these freedoms because they each gave their one life for us.

Now it's our turn. It is time to honor the sacrifice of these Legends of Liberty by living out the freedom for which they were willing to die.

Stop taking it for granted. Stop saying that someone else will "take care of it."

Start looking for ways that you can give of yourself, invest your one life, into causes greater than yourself.

Start living in such a way that, like Nathan Hale, your only regret will be that you do not have more lives to give.

Start living like a Legend of Liberty.

---

[1] There are several accounts of Nathan Hale's speech and much disagreement over his exact words. Whether he said "one life to lose" or "one life to give" or "if I had 10,000 lives, I would lay them all down" or some other version, it is indisputable that all accounts confirm the same theme. This young man believed he was doing his duty, that his cause was just, and he had absolutely zero hesitation about paying the ultimate price so that you and I could have the freedom we enjoy today.

LEGEND 2

WENTWORTH CHESWELL

VOICED BY:
DAVID BARTON

The legend of Wentworth Cheswell is told by David Barton.

David Barton is, by far, the foremost living expert on the Founding Fathers of America. His library of over 100,000 original documents is the largest known private collection of founding era sources. The socialist leaning history revisionists of today are constantly frustrated by David's publications that bring people back to the original sources and actual words of America's Founders. He may be a thorn in the side of the left, but he has been a breath of fresh air to an entire generation of freedom loving Americans who wish to pass that freedom in tact to their children. Visit WallBuilders.com to discover a wealth of information and book David to speak to your community.

I have had the privilege of learning from David for more than fifteen years. As a speaker for WallBuilders and host of David's daily radio program (visit WallBuildersLive.com for station listings or streaming), I regularly witness his encyclopedic knowledge of the Founders and the principles upon which America was built. Even more interesting than David's wealth of knowledge regarding well known founders like Washington and Jefferson, is when he shares the great contributions of unknown founders.

Wentworth Cheswell is a Legend of Liberty who greatly influenced the founding of America.

- Rick Green

Black Revolutionary Era Patriot
(1746-1817)

At WallBuilders we strive to "present America's forgotten history and heroes, with an emphasis on our moral, religious, and constitutional heritage," so Wentworth Cheswell (sometimes Chiswell or Cheswill) is a perfect subject for our attention.

He was the grandson of black slave Richard Cheswell (who early gained his freedom and in 1717 and became the first black to own property in the colony of New Hampshire); and he was the son of Hopestill Cheswell, a notable homebuilder who built the homes of several patriot leaders, including John Paul Jones and the Rev. Samuel Langdon. Wentworth was named after the famous Wentworth family, from whom came several state governors, including Benning Wentworth – the governor at the time of Wentworth's birth.

In 1763, Wentworth began attending an academy in Byfield, Massachusetts (30 miles from his home), where for four years he received an extensive education, studying Latin, Greek, swimming, horsemanship, reading, writing, and arithmetic.

In 1767, he returned home and became a schoolteacher, also marrying Mary Davis (they eventually had 13 children – 4 sons and 9 daughters). At the age of 21, he had already become an established and educated property owner and a stalwart in his local church, even holding a church pew.

The following year, Wentworth was elected town constable – the first of many offices he held throughout his life. Two years later in 1770, he was elected town selectman (the selectmen were considered the "town fathers" of a community). Other town offices in which he served included seven years as Auditor, six years as Assessor, two years as Coroner, seven years as town Moderator (presiding over town meetings), and twelve years as Justice of the Peace, overseeing trials, settling disputes, and executing deeds, wills, and legal documents. For half a century – including every year from 1768 until 1817 – Wentworth held some position in local government.

In addition to his civic service, Wentworth was also a patriot leader. In fact, the town selected him as the messenger for the Committee of Safety – the central nervous system of the American Revolution that carried intelligence and messages back and forth between strategic operational centers. Serving in that position, Wentworth undertook the same task as Paul Revere, making an all-night ride to warn citizens of imminent British invasion.

In April 1776, he signed a document in which he pledged, "at the risk of . . . live and fortune," to take up arms to resist the

British, and in September 1777, he enlisted in a company of Light Horse Volunteers commanded by Colonel John Langdon (Langdon later became one of the 55 Founding Fathers who drafted the U. S. Constitution, then a framer of the Bill of Rights, and later the New Hampshire governor). Langdon's company made a 250-mile march to Saratoga, New York, to join with the Continental Army under General Horatio Gates to defeat British General Burgoyne at the Battle of Saratoga – the first major American victory in the Revolution.

After returning from Saratoga, in the spring of 1778, Wentworth was elected to the convention to draft the state's first constitution, but some unknown event prevented his attendance.

Wentworth also served as Newmarket's unofficial historian, copying town records from 1727 (including the records of various church meetings) and chronicling old stories of the town as well as its current events. Additionally, having investigated and made extensive notes on numerous artifacts and relics he discovered in the region around Newmarket, he is considered the state's first archeologist. Therefore, when the Rev. Jeremy Belknap published his famous three-volume History of New Hampshire (1784-1792), he relied on (and openly acknowledged) much information he gleaned from Wentworth.

In 1801, Wentworth helped start the town library to preserve and disseminate useful knowledge and virtue. His commitment to providing helpful information is not surprising, for not only had he become a school teacher in 1767 but in 1776 he was elected as one of five men to regulate and oversee the schools of Newmarket.

In 1817, in his 71st year of age, Wentworth succumbed to typhus fever and was buried on the family farm, where other members of his family were later buried. In fact, when his daughter Martha died (his last surviving heir), her will provided that any members or descendants of the family could forever forward be buried on the farm. Unfortunately, that family graveyard long lay in disrepair, but in recent years friends and family have managed to restore it.

The legacy of Wentworth Cheswell is a lasting one: a patriot, teacher, and church leader; an historian, archeologist, and educator; a judge and official elected to numerous offices (he is considered the first black American elected to office in America). He is truly one of our forgotten patriots but he is a laudable example for all Americans – a hero worth remembering and honoring.

Sources:

William C. Nell, *The Colored Patriots of the American Revolution, With Sketches of Several Distinguished Colored Persons: To Which is Added a Brief Survey of the Conditions and Prospects of Colored Americans* (Boston: Robert F. Wallcut, 1855), pp. 120-121.

Sidney and Emma Nogrady Kaplan, *The Black Presence in the Era of the American Revolution, Revised Edition* (Amherst: The University of Massachusetts Press, 1989), pp. 200-202.

Thomas Truxtun Moebs, *Black Soldiers-Black Sailors-Black Ink: Research Guide on African-Americans in U.S. Military History, 1526-1900* (Chesapeake Bay: Moebs Publishing Company, 1994), pp. 226, 259, 280.

LEGEND

3

SQUANTO

VOICED BY:
GARY NEWELL

The legend of Squanto is told by Gary Newell.

Gary is a former professional football player. After football, he was called to youth ministry and founded Outreach America (for more information, visit OutreachAmerica.org). Gary has spoken to over a million young people on four continents and ministers across the globe at camps, conferences, and churches. He is also a successful business owner passionate about sharing lessons on integrity, teamwork, and unity.

Gary and I together dreamed up the idea of this book more than three years ago. We both love history and heroes and we love telling stories. We ~~steal~~ borrow each other's material all the time, but don't tell Gary. I think that he thinks it's been a one-way street and doesn't know I've been borrowing his stories too! You can follow Gary at twitter.com/GaryNewell.

I'm excited about the very unique style in which Gary has written this chapter. It's an art form of story telling I've never seen in a book before and I believe you are going to enjoy it!

Squanto is a Legend of Liberty used miraculously by God to prepare the way for the seeds of liberty to be sowed by the Pilgrims.

- Rick Green

PREFACE.

Who needs a preface for a chapter?

I DO!

I love to hear great stories...I love to tell great stories. As you will see, my writing style is a little "out of the box" ...not the expected form. Rather than perfect literary prose, I prefer to tell the story... as though we are sitting together in a small group.

> In fact... picture yourself in a log cabin
> nestled deep in the woods.
> A fire is blazing in the fireplace.
> Between the crackle of the burning logs, we
> can faintly hear the lake's small waves lap up on
> the lake's shoreline. You've got your favorite
> coffee, espresso, energy drink...

(I'm an energy drink guy)...

> Fresh snow is beginning to fall...
> and as we sit around with a few friends,

I begin to tell this story.

I have a special request for my chapter...read it out loud. Yes, out loud. This story needs to be HEARD. Trust me, it's much better that way.

So, with that being said...are you ready?

My Preface is complete. Let's begin... out loud, please.

Daniel Webster once wrote, *"History is God's providence in human affairs."*

I believe this story is one of the greatest testimonies to Webster's statement ever recorded.

The year was 1605... (that is for my friends that are familiar with my talks).

This is the incredible story of a Patuxet Indian named Tisquantum... stop, stop, stop...

I know... that's the first name in the story and you can't even pronounce it.

Okay, let me start over.

That was his given tribal Indian name, but he was also known by the explorers, and the historians, as Squanto.

Squanto was born between 1580 and 1590 (the exact date is not known). He lived near the present-day town of Plymouth,

Massachusetts. Nothing is known about his early life, except that he was a member of the Patuxet Tribe that lived in eastern Massachusetts.

The Patuxet tribe was part of a larger tribe known as the Wampanoag. During the early part of the seventeenth century, the Wampanoag tribe covered much of the New England territory.

Squanto did NOT spend his early years living in a teepee. Instead, he was raised in a wetus, which is the Wampanoag word for house.

...I know what you're thinking, "What's so important about that?"

Actually, nothing.

It's just interesting. C'mon, be honest, you have no idea what a wetus is!

A wetus was a small house. It was usually 8-10 feet tall, made of a wooden frame covered with woven mats and sheets of birch bark. The frame was shaped like a dome, a cone, or a rectangle, with an arched roof...
...and that would have been "home."

Squanto would have eaten what was called the "Three Sisters"... maize, beans, and squash.

...today we call it a vegetable plate.

The Patuxet Indians were hunter-gatherers and skilled fisherman. As a boy Squanto learned these skills.

Back to 1605...

That's when the adventure begins!

Squanto and four other Indian braves were captured by Captain George Weymouth.

Weymouth was commissioned to explore the New England coast by Sir Ferdinando Gorges, the owner of the Plymouth Company.

Captain Weymouth reportedly captured the young braves so he could present them to financial backers in Britain.

In other words, to show them off and impress the "money" guys.

Let's put this into perspective...

These five braves were bound by chains and iron shackles, and locked in the bottom cell of Weymouth's ship. Can you imagine the horror of that experience?

The seasickness, the vomiting, the stench, the constipation, and the fevers.
I think they would have welcomed death.

Adding to the bad conditions were hunger and thirst. They

were only given small portions of sharply salted rations, bug infested hard biscuits, a bit of moldy cheese, and foul water.

...no more "Three Sisters" for sure.

...and the length of a trans-Atlantic voyage varied from 47 to 138 days!

Imagine how those young Patuxet braves felt as they adjusted their eyes to the bright sunlight when they finally walked down the plank to the dock...

...in a country of pale-skinned people, who wore clothes, and didn't speak their native tongue.

I'm sure they believed they would never see their family or tribe again.

We don't know the fate of the other four braves who were captured by Captain Weymouth, but as for Squanto, this is where all the "God's providence" story was just beginning.

Sir Ferdinando Gorges brought Squanto to live with him.

Gorges taught Squanto the English language, which he later became fluent in. Gorges also introduced him to many of his "explorer" friends.

One of those friends was Captain John Smith...

...Smith was famous for having been rescued by Pocahontas at the Jamestown Colony, several years earlier.

Captain Smith was looking for another command so he could return to New England (which, by the way, he named), on a mapping and exploring voyage.

In 1614, Smith got his expedition.

Squanto had been in England for nine years.

He had spent hours educating Sir Gorges on the tribes that populated the Atlantic coast. He told him where they were located, and the most favorable places to establish colonies.

This information was fascinating and valuable to John Smith, so he asked Gorges, and was granted permission, to take Squanto to New England with him.

Squanto served as Smith's guide and interpreter. Once the expedition was completed, Captain Smith promised, Squanto would be free to return to his people.

(Here is that "God's providence" thing again)

Two ships set sail from Great Britain. One was captained by John Smith, and the other by British explorer, Captain Thomas Hunt.

Squanto fulfilled his obligations to Captain Smith, and as promised, he was set free.

While enjoying the woods he once hunted with friends, Squanto came across Captain Thomas Hunt.

Captain Hunt decided to stay behind, after John Smith left for England. He told Smith that he was going to gather more profitable beaver pelts before he returned...

But that wasn't exactly true... Hunt had other plans.

As they talked, Captain Hunt convinced Squanto to bring twenty of the young Patuxet braves on board his ship to barter.

Once on board, Hunt promptly clapped them in iron shackles.

He then sailed across the bay to the outer edge of Cape Cod where he captured seven more braves from the Nauset Tribe.

Captain Hunt stored the Indians below the hatches. He sailed through the Straits of Gibraltar to the city of Malaga, Spain, a notorious slave trading port, where he sold as many as he could.

However, local monks in Malaga learned that the Indians were brought from America, so they took custody of the remaining braves...

...which just happened to include Squanto.
(yes, that "God's providence" thing... again)

The monks took good care of Squanto. They also felt it was their responsibility to teach him the Christian faith.

After a short period, the monks arranged for Squanto to return to England.

Remember Daniel Webster's quote?

"History is God's providence in human affairs."

Listen to this "coincidence."

(...and if you actually believe this is all a "coincidence"... hang on... I'm about to introduce you to "providence.")

Once in England, Squanto began living with Sir John Slanie, in Cornhill, London.

Slanie was the treasurer of the Newfoundland Company, and he employed Squanto as an interpreter and an expert on North American natural resources.

(I think he was qualified for the job, since he was the only one who actually lived in North America, don't you?)

Slanie sent Squanto to Newfoundland to work with the governor of the Newfoundland Colony, Captain John Mason.

Stay with me... follow this...

While working for Governor Mason, Squanto was introduced to a ship's captain by the name of Thomas Dermer.

Keep hanging...

Dermer was employed by the New England Company, which was headed by none other than, Sir Ferdinando Gorges.

Small world, huh!

It gets smaller...

Dermer worked with Captain John Smith, and is believed to have been on Smith's 1614 voyage to New England.

Gorges was passionate about beaver trade with the Indians of Massachusetts.

There just happened to be a small problem...

The Nauset and Patuxet tribes were outraged by Captain Hunt's kidnapping of those 27 braves. In fact, they became very hostile. English and French ships were no longer welcome in New England.

One French captain and crew had their ship burned, and almost everyone on board was killed by the Nauset, in 1617.

So, obviously, the profitable beaver trade had stopped.

Thomas Dermer sent a letter to his boss, Sir Ferdinando Gorges, explaining that Squanto could act as an interpreter and peacemaker between the English and the enraged Patuxet and Nauset tribes. Squanto could open up beaver trade once again.

They met with Gorges and he liked their plan.

In 1619, Captain Dermer and Squanto set sail for New England.

Their goals... make peace, re-establish trade, and map out the natural resources.

Now, pause for a moment and let's re-cap the story...

Squanto was captured in 1605...

Taken to England, where he lived for nine years...

Returned to his people in 1614, but was immediately kidnapped again and taken to Spain to be sold into slavery...

Rescued by local monks...

Sent to England where he was employed by a man who sent him to Newfoundland...

A Captain who had been with him on the 1614 voyage to New England then employed him for the next year...

That Captain convinced Squanto's first English employer to send them back to New England...

In 1619, after being gone for fourteen years... Squanto sailed home again!

...That is what is known as "God's providence."

...but it's not over yet!

After they reached New England, Dermer anchored at Monhegan, one of the major fishing stations in Maine.

Hang on... this is important...

It was here that Dermer picked up Samoset, chief of the Algonquins. Samoset had been in the area for the past eight months. He begged a ride down the coast and Captain Dermer dropped both Squanto and Samoset off at Plymouth.

We'll get back to Samoset later...

After fourteen years Squanto was finally back in his homeland. Imagine the excitement he must have felt as he stood on that seashore and began the trek inland to greet his people.

However, that homecoming never happened.

Three years earlier, a mysterious plague had come through and killed every man, woman, and child. All that remained were skulls, bones, and tattered remnants of ruined dwellings.

Squanto was the only living Patuxet Indian on planet earth.

Squanto drifted aimlessly through the woods and fields some fifty miles to the southwest, where he came upon the camp of the Wampanoag tribe, led by their wise chief, Massasoit.

Massasoit took the lonely brave in and made him part of their tribe.

The year is now 1620... let me change the scene...

Men, women, and children (102 in total) were packed into the lower deck of a tiny ship called the Mayflower.

Most were farmers from Scewby, England.

King James ran them out of England, because they felt the Church of England was corrupt.

They were known as Separatists.

For twelve years they lived in northern Holland.

Though they enjoyed religious freedom in Holland, they had become concerned for their children.

Their vision was to found a nation...
...a Christian nation.

They formed the Mayflower Compact, which declared that..

"We whose names are underwritten, having undertaken for the glory of God, and advancement of the Christian faith...a voyage to plant the first colony in the northern parts of Virginia."

They purchased two boats, the Mayflower and the Speedwell. However, the Speedwell had a leak, so they had to abandon it.

They all crammed into the Mayflower, which was ninety feet long, twenty-five feet wide, and had about five and a half feet of headroom.

Due to storms and torrential downpours, they remained below deck for sixty-six days and nights.

No one was allowed on deck.

They were forced to sleep on the floor.
There was very little light or air.
There were no bathrooms.
They wore the same clothes for the entire voyage.

Food was salted fish, beef, pork, and a hardtack, which was just a hard, dry biscuit. Water was contaminated.

Seasickness abounded.

The average loss of life on any trans-Atlantic voyage at that time was fifty percent.

...yet no Pilgrims died.
(You got it... "God's providence")

In fact, there were only two who died on that voyage.

One was a man who continually made fun of their faith. He caught a mysterious fever and died.

The other was the servant of the Captain. He didn't drink lime and died of scurvy.

One of the passengers was a gentleman named John Holland.

He couldn't handle being below deck any longer and decided to lift the hatch and step on the deck to get some fresh air.

I don't blame him.

I can't even comprehend how bad the stench must have been.

As soon as Holland reached the deck, the storm tossed him into the Atlantic.

For perspective... a man can survive for about four minutes in the north Atlantic in November.

...so here it comes... more of "God's providence..."

As Holland surfaced, a rope from the back of the boat happened to cross his wrist. He quickly wrapped his arm around it and was pulled to safety.

John Holland went on to become a leading elder in the colony.

Coincidence?

Those "coincidences" are really adding up...

I believe that is yet another example of "God's providence in human affairs."
...and here comes another one...

The Mayflower was originally headed to northern Virginia, as the Mayflower Compact recorded.

However, every time they tried to enter the area, storms and strong winds came out of nowhere, and forced the ship north.

Finally, the Captain decided to land where the storm subsided.

On November 20, 1620, the Mayflower landed at Cape Cod, Massachusetts.

...once again, "God's providence."

You see, the plague that had wiped out the entire Patuxet nation had also frightened every neighboring tribe. No other Indians would enter that area for fear of the plague.

The storms and winds had blown that tiny ship to the only safe haven on the entire east coast.

Had the Mayflower landed at any other location, those outraged tribes would have slaughtered every one in the colony.

As the Pilgrims reached the shore, their knees hit the sand and they claimed this land as the first (and only) nation ever founded as a Christian nation.

However... the real challenges were just beginning.
They had arrived in late November. It was too late to plant crops.

By February, fifty percent of the Pilgrims had died from the harsh winter, starvation, and disease.

The only ones remaining were:

> 22 men
> 4 married women
> 5 adolescent girls
> 9 adolescent boys
> 13 young children

Can you handle yet another instance of "God's providence?"
This is going to be good.

Pause for a moment... give your voice a break.

I need you to put yourself IN this next setting. You need to
FEEL this one.

Ok... here we go.

> Picture this...

It's Friday, March 16, 1621...

> It is a fair, warm, but slightly windy day.
> Winter is beginning to subside.

You are one of the twenty-two men remaining in the colony.

You are seated in the Common House with all of the other
men. You have all spent the morning planning your military
defense for the colony. You look across the table at a group of
great, godly men, who have laid it all on the line for this ideal...

Founding a Christian nation!

You look into the eyes of William Bradford, John Holland, Stephen Hopkins, Miles Standish, and the colony's spiritual leader, William Brewster, to name a few. There's a solemn mood in the room because each of you knows the peril you face as spring approaches. To a man, you all know how few and weak you are, and what easy prey you will be, if attacked.

Suddenly a cry rings out... "Indian coming!"

You couldn't have heard that right... "Indian coming?"

The other men have the same puzzled look.

You know he must have meant to say, "Indians coming."

Captain Standish heads to the window...with one look, he opens the door and moves to the street. You jump from your seat and follow. All the men file into the street behind you.

(Ok... FEEL this...)

You stand, startled, and see walking boldly toward you, one tall, well-built Indian.

He is virtually naked, wearing only a fringed loincloth around his waist and moccasins on his feet. He carries his bow, an empty quiver, and in his hand he holds two arrows.

He has come alone, stops before you and salutes... then comes the greatest shock since landing on these shores...

In a deep, resonant voice the Indian clearly says ...

"Welcome, Englishmen!"

As a group, you are too astounded to speak.
Did this just happen?
Who is he?
What is he doing here?

His name is... Samoset!
(I told you we would get back to him.)

Samoset!

Can you imagine the feeling? An Indian brave appears out of the woods speaking English.

Really?

Yes, yes, and yes!
(I think we can call it..."God's providence.")

Chief Massasoit had been secretly watching the Pilgrims. He decided to send Samoset to meet them because he spoke some English.

While Squanto spent fourteen years in captivity in Spain and England, Samoset had been living on Monhegan Island. He had learned English from his contact with the English fishermen and traders who visited that region.

Though he spoke a broken English, it was sufficient to provide the Pilgrims with information about the land,

the people,
the places,
the distances,
and most importantly...
information about the Wampanoag tribe and Chief Massasoit.

Samoset spent the night with the Pilgrims. He left the next morning carrying a knife, a ring, and a bracelet, as gifts for Chief Massasoit.

Five days later, on Thursday, March 22, 1621, Samoset returned to the colonists accompanied by a special companion...

Squanto!

Squanto brought Chief Massasoit to meet the colonists. He eventually established a treaty between the colony and the Wampanoag tribe that lasted for forty years.

The Pilgrims settled in Patuxet, the site of Squanto's old village.

Squanto knew that they couldn't survive much longer before starvation would wipe out the colony. He began immediately teaching them to plant corn, the Indian way, and to plant pumpkins among the corn, to stalk deer, and to trap beaver. He showed them all the best places to fish, and how to make maple syrup from the sap of maple trees.

Squanto never left the Pilgrims. He was their friend, guide, and interpreter.

He had found his purpose.

In October, Governor William Bradford declared a day of public thanksgiving. Chief Massasoit was invited and brought ninety Indians with him. He also brought the first Thanksgiving meal, which included five deer, more than a dozen turkeys, and Indian corn.

For three days they feasted, played games, and gave thanks to God for His divine providence.

According to the diary of Pilgrim Governor William Bradford...

Squanto "became a special instrument sent of God for [our] good . . ."

When Squanto lay dying of a fever in November 1623, Bradford wrote that their Indian friend "desir[ed] the Governor to pray for him, that he might go to the Englishmen's God in heaven."

Squanto bequeathed his possessions to his English friends "as remembrances of his love."

As Daniel Webster once wrote, *"History is God's providence in human affairs."*

Hopefully, you realize that what you've just seen is that truth played out in the life of one Patuxet Indian, and a remaining colony of Pilgrims whose lives, dreams, and cause, were rescued from extinction.

A good story is entertaining.

A great story teaches a life lesson.

...This is a great story.

So stay with me for just a bit longer... you're almost done, but this is the most important part of the story.

You can stop reading out loud now... you did good though!

I want to leave you with two simple lessons.

First... Squanto's story is the story of "God's providence" in his life, and in our nation.

There is no denying that God's miraculous Hand was upon the events that took place in the initial founding of America. The story of Squanto and that Plymouth colony is one miracle after another.

America did not happen by accident.

It was, and still remains, the first and only nation founded as a Christian nation. The intent and ideal were spelled out very clearly in the Mayflower Compact, as well as in further writings of those original colonists.

That vision remained consistent in the writings of our Founding Fathers, in both the Declaration of Independence and the Constitution.

Sadly, those intentions, ideals, and visions are becoming very clouded in today's society.

In fact, today, we live in the most hostile environment, in regards to our religious freedoms and liberties, that has existed in our nation since November 20, 1620.

We are in a battle between two opposing worldviews.

One leads to liberty.
The other leads to statism.

If liberty wins...
the statists will live alongside us in a free and prosperous country, which rests on the foundations of our Constitutional Republic and a Judeo-Christian worldview.

If the statists win...
we will become subjects of their government,
not citizens of a republic,
and the light of a free America will go out forever.

If America is not an accident...
then the question becomes...

Is God through with America?

I don't think so... but our freedom is fragile!

The answer to the battle lies within the second lesson we take from our story.

Secondly... one life can make a difference.

The story of Squanto is the story of the difference one life makes.

Once Squanto met the Pilgrims... living in his homeland...
...it was said that he found his purpose.

Fourteen years of pain, separation, loss, and utter confusion were part of preparing him for that purpose...

...and his one life made a difference.

Who would have thought that the only living Patuxet Indian would be the little known, seemingly insignificant life that God used to save a nation?

I believe with every fiber of my being that the same God we saw in those "God providences" of this chapter, is still at work today in the lives of ordinary people like you and me.

You are not insignificant. You can make a difference.

No, no...

You HAVE to make a difference. We HAVE to make a difference, together.

If the American republic is to be restored...
If America is to be great once again...

It will not occur because professional politicians woke up to reality.

It will occur because...you, me...WE wake up and remember a forgotten truth...

You, Me...We...
are the guardians of this Constitutional Republic...
and the power to restore it lies within us.

LEGEND 4

JACKIE
ROBINSON

VOICED
BY:
BRAD
STINE

The legend of Jackie Robinson is told by Brad Stine.

Brad is the most media covered Christian comic in America. He frequently guest stars on our history/reality television program, *Chasing American Legends*. Brad's comedy has you laughing out loud one minute, and pondering the most important things in life the very next. Brad and I often team up for the Comedy & Constitution Tour, where we entertain and educate audiences on the foundations of America and the duty of citizens to preserve freedom for future generations. Visit www.ComedyConstitution.com for more information on bringing the event to your community and visit www.BradStine.com to book Brad or purchase his hilarious DVD's.

Brad chose Jackie Robinson because, like all the Green boys, Brad was a baseball player and has great respect for those who reach the top of a profession that involves what is universally accepted as the most difficult action in all of sports – hitting a 90+ mph small round ball with a round bat!

Jackie Robinson is a Legend of Liberty, not because of his baseball feats alone, but because his sacrifice, suffering, perseverance, and excellence led the way to liberty for an entire race of people.

His story is legendary in sports, but also legendary in the annals of liberty.

- Rick Green

A True Hero

> *"A life is not important,*
> *except in the impact it has on other lives."*
> - Jackie Robinson

I am a comedian by profession. If you don't know who I am, it means either you are unsophisticated regarding the "pros" of the live comedy world, or I am really a "nobody." (The second option is probably most likely!)

As a comedian I am a purveyor of words. I like them. I use them all the time. Words matter to me—they can make or break my career. But words are important to all of us, no matter what our profession. Words give meaning to life. They define the way we think, personally, and as a society. I would even go as far as to say, whoever controls the language, controls the world. For that reason, we need to choose our words carefully, and never abuse or overuse them.

Hero is one word, in my opinion, that has been used in such a cavalier way that its meaning and power have been totally diluted.

he·ro `hirō/
noun

1. A person, typically a man, who is admired or idealized
for: courage, outstanding achievements, or noble qualities.
(By the way, heroine is the female form of hero.)

The problem is that our society uses this word a little too loosely today. For example, heroes are all over the evening news. Recently both a man who risked his life to rescue a dog from the middle of a frozen lake, and a boy who found a wallet that wasn't his and returned it without asking for a reward, were both heralded as heroes. Are they really both heroes? Take another look at the definition, if you are unsure.

Something is wrong when a culture has reached a point that simply doing the right thing (like returning a wallet that is not yours) is considered an act of heroism. When a society defines such behavior as heroic, it's an indication that they have lost their way.

By definition true heroes are rare, but they do exist. I know, because I have a hero in my life. He is someone I have admired since childhood. The way he lived his life inspires the way I live and work today. He's not just my hero though, he's America's hero. His achievements have changed our nation, and the world. His name is Jackie Robinson, and I am going to share a little of how his life fulfilled the definition of what it means to be a hero.

I am a Los Angeles Dodgers fan. I have been one since I was three years old. I remember sitting on my dad's lap and listening to Dodgers games on the radio. True Dodgers fan are defined not only by their love for the Dodgers but by their complete hatred of the San Francisco Giants. (Diehard fans hate the New York Yankees, even more.)

One of the greatest benefits of growing up as a true Dodgers fan was the opportunity it provided me to learn about the proud history of the franchise, especially in regard to its most important player of all time, Jackie Robinson. Robinson was the first Negro major league baseball player of the modern era. Yet, even more amazing is that Jackie Robinson broke baseball's "color barrier," in 1947.

Most true baseball fans know the story of Jackie Robinson, but what they may not realize, especially today, is that he was one of the first to shift the momentum of our country with regards to racism. As you are about to discover, he was among the first to blaze a trail that ultimately led to an improved quality of life for millions of American citizens.

I admire the courage it must have taken for Jackie Robinson to rise up and face the challenges of his day. I also realize how difficult it is for me to understand and relate to the amount of opposition he faced. As a professional athlete he would have had to outperform his peers, simply because of the color of his skin. He succeeded in doing that even while being physically and emotionally abused, sometimes by his own teammates. Robinson had the discipline to meet and exceed every expectation placed on him. His accomplishments are almost unprecedented in American history. By every definition of the word, he is a true American hero.

Where did he draw the strength to endure and ultimately succeed at shattering stereotypes that had undergirded racism for generations in America? What kind of a man was Jackie Robinson?

Jackie was born in Cairo, Georgia on January 31, 1919. He was the son of sharecroppers. Shortly after his birth his family moved to Pasadena, California. Robinson's mother Mallie, was the one who instilled a strong belief in God, in all of her five children. The greatest lesson she taught them was that God would take care of their lives and provide for all their needs. "I never stopped believing that," Robinson later said.

Chris Lamb writes,

> *"It took awhile for Robinson as a young man to understand what that faith in God meant. He was involved in more than one fight, and scrapes with the law, prompted by racial antagonism."*

In his 1997 Robinson biography, Arnold Rampersad, describes how Jackie was rescued from the streets as a teenager by the Reverand Karl Downs. Down's was the minister of Scott United Methodist Church in Pasadena. He became a father figure to Robinson and ultimately brought him back into the church.

Downs was the channel through which religious faith "finally flowed into Jack's consciousness and was finally accepted there, if on revised terms, as he himself reached manhood," Mr. Rampersad writes. "Faith in God then began to register in him as both a mysterious force, beyond his comprehension, and a pragmatic way to negotiate the world." From that point in his life, Robinson made praying beside his bed a daily habit.

A few years later Robinson attended UCLA where his athletic gifts did not go unnoticed. He became the first student in UCLA history to earn a letter in four different sports in the same season.

Though best known for breaking the color barrier in baseball, Jackie's entire life was lived on the frontlines in the war against bigotry and prejudice. Long before he became a household name, he was making a difference. One such instance occurred while Jackie was in the military.

On July 6, 1944, while returning on a non-segregated military bus from an evening at the Colored Officers Club, Jackie took a seat next to the wife of another officer, who, although black, appeared white to the bus driver. The driver stopped the bus and ordered Robinson to go to the back of the bus. He refused. The bus driver was a superior officer, so Jackie was arrested for disobeying his direct order. He ultimately stood to be court martialed for the charge. The decision rested in the hands of nine men (eight white and one black). Despite the odds, Robinson was acquitted. Jackie Robinson fought for his rights long before it came into the forefront of national attention, and almost a decade before Rosa Parks made headlines by refusing to move to the back of a bus in Montgomery, Alabama.

I am especially humbled and in awe of Robinson because he not only stood for his rights as an American, but the rights of all black Americans. He did it alone, and at a time when the culture was not sympathetic to his plight. His stance could have literally cost him his life. He was a strong Christian, and a true American hero. He opposed those who were trying to steal his God-given freedom. We desperately need to see that kind courage and heroics today. Not only to inspire us as a nation, but quite frankly to remind us that it can still be done.

Although America remains the greatest nation in the world, things are beginning to shift. We live in an age where

Christianity is being maligned, attacked, ridiculed, and intentionally purged from recorded history. The truth is, Christianity has played a major role throughout our national history. It was the guiding principle behind the thoughts and ideas of those who founded and shaped our nation. Judeo-Christian values have largely been responsible for creating societies that promote dignity and defend individual rights, around the world.

The underlying story of Robinson's legacy is rarely told. Few today know that he was a strong Christian, and that his achievements were directly connected to his beliefs. But Jackie always credited his faith in God for carrying him through the grueling ordeal of integrating the major leagues. He knew the chief purpose of a Christian's life is to know God and to make Him known, and that is what motivated him, and gave him the courage, to live the way he did.

Jackie's resolve was constantly challenged, but he held his ground and stood for what was right. He did it within the context of our American value system, which guarantees each person's unalienable right to, "Life, Liberty, and the Pursuit of happiness." Those immutable truths are the framework of our freedom. They were established by our Founding Fathers who declared them to be given to all men, by their Creator.

The Founders of our nation fought and won their independence from an oppressive government. They understood the evil nature of humanity. When they established the laws of our new nation, they did so knowing that if institutional safeguards were not put into place, the day would likely come when those governing would once again try to steal the freedoms of those being governed. They knew that despite the victory they were experiencing, cultural mores could shift, and America's newfound freedom would erode. So they created a system that gave a voice to the people and would enable them to resist such changes in the future. Jackie Robinson was one of those voices.

Martin Luther King was another whose voice was heard. When King began to march and demand that our government take its creed seriously, both his home and his brother's, were bombed. His life was ultimately taken for the cause. Despite it all, King's legacy is one of unity. He brought solidarity among large groups of black and white Americans, who were ready and willing to march alongside of him. I'm sure there was a sense of impending danger at every turn, but that didn't stop King. His courage and legacy is rightly deserved. Like Robinson, King was a strong Christian and a great American hero.

Both men impacted our nation, but while Martin Luther King had the advantage of having large numbers who stood by his side, Jackie Robinson stood alone. No one stood with him, and no one preceded him.

As Henry Louis Gates, Jr. wrote:

> "To understand the even broader social and political import of what Robinson's actions on the field initiated, we need only consider the chain reaction of crucial episodes in the history of the civil rights movement that unfolded almost immediately after his first season with the Dodgers."

> First, President Harry Truman issued Executive Order 9982 on July 26, 1948, just over a year after Robinson faced his first

pitcher at Ebbets Field, abolishing racial discrimination in the armed forces. It is certainly reasonable to assume that Truman's timing was informed by Robinson's successful integration of professional baseball. Truman's desegregation of the military no doubt informed the Supreme Court's Brown v. Board decision desegregating public schools in 1954, which in turn informed the actions of Rosa Parks on her bus, leading to the Montgomery Bus Boycott. Out of the Montgomery Bus Boycott emerged the leadership role of the young Martin Luther King Jr. Without Martin Luther King, Jr. there would have been no modern civil rights movement."

Robinson rose to the challenge by outperforming at the top level of his sport. As a rookie, playing for a storied franchise, he was despised by most of the players. Yet, the greatest challenge for Robinson had to be keeping the promise that he made to General Manager, Branch Rickey, when he brought Jackie onto the team.

Rickey was also a deeply committed Christian. Even though he was the General Manager of the Dodgers, he refused to attend games on Sunday. One day he brought Robinson into his office to propose his intention. He wanted to use Jackie Robinson to break the color barrier. He knew Robinson had the talent, and wanted to be sure that he also had the strength of character to go all the way. Branch showed Jackie a book that was published in the 1920s by Giovanni Papini, and titled, simply, "Life of Christ." He read Jesus' words to Robinson, *"But whoever shall smite thee on the cheek, turn to him the other also."*

Rickey spoke to Robinson about what it would take for him to succeed in the face of the great opposition he would encounter. He explained that the only way to win was not to respond to those indignities. He believed that unless Jackie did what Jesus instructed, and turned the other cheek, he would fail.

Both men rightly understood the violence that would be unleashed, but at first Robinson was a bit confused by Rickey's suggestion. Jackie was not afraid to stand up for his rights when confronted, and believed that was exactly what would be needed. "Mr. Rickey" he said, "Do you want a ballplayer who's afraid to fight back?"

Rickey's reply raised the bar. "No" said Rickey, "I'm looking for a ballplayer with guts enough not to fight back."

Branch Rickey believed Robinson's faith would give him the spiritual depth to discern that what he suggested was what was required. After a moment, Robinson replied, "I have two cheeks, Mr. Rickey. Is that it?"

Ultimately, it was this short meeting between two strong Christian men, Branch Rickey and Jackie Robinson, that changed baseball, and America, forever.

Christianity is unique because it transforms men and women from the inside out. Believers know that the way to be a true warrior for Christ is through quiet, sacrificial love, even towards our enemies. To be afraid to fight back is indeed cowardice, but to choose not to fight back for a greater good, is courage. Courage, I might add, beyond human nature.

Try to imagine what it was like for Jackie Robinson. How did he feel when pitchers threw balls at his head? What did it take for him to dust himself off and run to first base? How was he able to perform at his highest level when at every game he was spiked, insulted, or spat upon? This was the majesty of the character of Jackie Robinson. He had a spiritual meekness that is rare, especially among professional athletes, and it helped him turn every adversity into an opportunity to try harder. He was truly one of baseball's greatest players.

Jackie Robinson honored his word to Branch Rickey. He never fought back physically, but he did fight back. He did it in a profound and unmistakable way—he outperformed! He allowed his skill to scream victoriously over his insulters. His dignified response triumphed over the bigotry he endured. He did it all in real time, on a baseball diamond, as the whole country watched and prayed. Some prayed for his success, others prayed for his failure. The results speak for themselves. Jackie Robinson won the rookie of the year award in the first year it was instituted, and went on to have one of the most amazing careers in baseball history.

There are three principles that I have learned from Jackie's life and I try to relate them to the way I live my life today. I believe they are lessons we can all apply.

⟁ LIFE LESSONS

1. We do not "own" our gift it is "loaned" to us. We all have at least one gift from God, and we can do one of two things with that gift. Either we can spend it on ourselves, or we can offer it back to God and ask Him to show us how to use that gift in our lives. I always felt that comedy was my livelihood, but in fact I realized, from Jackie Robinson's example, that comedy is a gift God has given me. It is the unique way in which he has equipped me to share His story with others. The same is true of each of us. We can waste our gifts by merely using them for ourselves, or we can choose to use them for God's Glory.

2. We often stand alone when speaking the truth. Scripture reminds us that we wrestle not against flesh and blood. Many people today allow themselves to be pawns in the enemy's game because they believe lies instead of truth. In Jackie Robinson's case the lie he stood against was something that had been deeply embedded in our American culture. The lie that some races are inferior to others has caused great damage. Whenever we believe a lie it affects how we live and relate to others. Lies deceive us and blind us because we are basing our actions on a false premise. Remember Jesus' prayer for those who nailed Him to the cross? He prayed for their forgiveness, saying that they did not know what they were doing. Jackie Robinson stood alone on the truth, and responded to opposition in the same way. A gentle response is often the most effective way to expose lies.

When I chose to stand for my Christian and conservative perspective through my comedy, I realized that any dream

I had for mainstream acceptance was more than likely over. But I believed my calling from God was unmistakable, and so I willingly chose to accept whatever resistance, hatred, and insults came my way. And they did come. Our culture is quickly becoming anti-Christian so when we live by His Word, we can expect to face opposition in this world. Jackie Robinson's example is an inspiration to continue to use the gifts God has given us to stand for truth in the face of opposition.

3. We may never see the result. Jackie Robinson died in 1972, and he was still asking why there were no black managers, general managers, or owners in baseball. He certainly saw progress, but it would not be until long after his death that America would see any black-owned sports teams, general managers, and managers. Jackie may have felt that his efforts had failed. But it's important to remember that the timing of the results is never in our hands. Our part is to follow God wherever He calls, and leave the results to Him.

I realize that, in my lifetime, I may never know if my career as a comedian has been of any benefit to fellow believers, or if any of the seeds that have been planted in the hearts of the searching will bear fruit. Only God knows those results.

Yet for myself, this is the gift Jackie's legacy gave to me. So if my life ends being even half the man he was, I WILL have lived a life that was important.

LEGEND 5

ZIG ZIGLAR

VOICED BY:
KRISH DHANAM

The legend of Zig Ziglar is told by international speaker/ trainer/author Krish Dhanam.

Krish came to America (legally!) with only $9 in his pocket. He now speaks to arenas filled with thousands of people, trains Fortune 500 companies, and leaves audiences everywhere spellbound with his wit and wisdom. Despite his high demand as a professional speaker, Krish has a servant's heart and continues to give of his time through Mala Ministries and frequently invests into the next generation by joining me in the training at Patriot Academy each summer.

As one of only two executive coaches personally trained by Zig Ziglar, Krish has successfully delivered his message of hope, humor and balance in over fifty countries and throughout the continental United States. His client list is the who's who of global enterprise and he has received accolades from some of the most distinguished organizations including, The United States Army, Christian Dior, Steelcase Industries, Apollo Hospitals, Weyerhauser and the Florida Department of Revenue.

He is the author of *The American Dream from an Indian Heart, From Abstracts to Absolutes* and contributing author to the book *Top Performance* written by Zig Ziglar. He co-authored *Hard Headed and Soft Hearted* with Rick Belluzzo (former President of Microsoft). Krish sits on the boards of Ravi Zacahrias Life Focus Society and Life Focus Knowledge Ventures Pvt. Ltd in India. As a Managing Partner in SkyLife Success he is constantly developing curriculum for global deployment. He is also actively involved in his church and is the President of Mala Ministeries. He and his bride Anila are the proud parents of Nicolas. Krish and his family make their home in Flower Mound, Texas.

Zig Ziglar is a Legend of Liberty who helped countless millions of people across the planet to apply the principles of liberty to their personal and professional lives, as well as their communities. I personally appreciate Krish contributing this chapter because Zig was a mentor to me as well. He was always a great supporter of my political campaigns and he wrote the foreword to my book, *Freedom's Frame*.

- Rick Green

Zig Ziglar
God's Salesman for America

*"The greatest good you can do for another is not just
share your riches, but reveal to him his own."*
- Benjamin Disraeli

The man on stage is electrifying the crowd. He is offering witty barbs and colloquialisms that make you scratch your head and wonder. His motivation is contagious and almost infectious. His accent is deeply Southern. His self-revealed identity--that of a flag waving, gung-ho American patriot. His demeanor is poised and confident. Part Billy Graham and part John Wayne, this man is quickly the crowd favorite. Then he reaches below the table and pulls out a shiny metal figure that seems to be bolted onto a wooden base. It looks like something you would find at the back of an abandoned farm house. The camera picks it up and shows it on the big screen. It's an old-fashioned water pump that he uses as a prop. Those that are familiar with him applaud with glee, while those that are new to him have a quizzical look. He eases their consternation by telling them what it is and then proceeds to dramatically and emotively tell a story that ties this pump to life, relationships, free enterprise, goal-setting, happiness and everything else.

67

A pump...really! In this day of technology and robots, email and instant messaging, digital photography and supersonic travel, a man uses a simple prop to connect the hopeless with dreams and the aimless with goals. The crowd stands when he is finished and rewards him for his message with a long, prolonged, standing ovation. He does this for the words--Well done my Good and Faithful Servant. He has been doing this for five decades. He is Zig Ziglar, an American icon, institution, and ideal, all wrapped in one.

Born into a large family in Coffee County, Alabama, the man who would change the lives of millions of people globally was actually left for dead as an infant when the doctors were sure he would not survive. A grandmother held him with love and prayed for deliverance and, just like Elijah was able to breathe new life into the widow's son, Hilary Hinton Ziglar was given a second chance. Most of the conquests from times of old to now have had at their heart great men who were birthed out of great sacrifice. Zig Ziglar was no different. But astronauts who took his messages to outer space and young immigrants who used his books to learn English will say he was anointed for a purpose. A different purpose. A purpose that would enable individuals and institutions that used his principles to flourish. A purpose cloaked in grace and bathed in mercy. A purpose that would meet the heart of the seeker and allow him to be sought. A purpose articulated in his own words as Confessions of a Happy Christian.

Growing up is hard but not harsh, as a wise mother instills duty by example and honor by affiliation. The boy becomes a young man and answers the call of a nation that is fighting the second global war. He does not see combat but begins to love the history of a nation and decides to incorporate the truth of the land he loves into his young sales career. Marriage will bring him a union with Jean Abernathy, whom he will call Sugar Baby in private and The Redhead in public for the rest of their married life. They will complement each other for over six decades as a couple and complete each other with four children as a family. He will become unique in sharing them with his audiences all over the world, thus giving each notoriety. What may have been an innocuous act of love is actually a profound principle of success and significance. Chronicled in Courtship after Marriage and Raising Positive Kids in a Negative World, these principles become instrumental in healing relationships and restoring the kindred of families all over the world. The uniqueness of his approach was that people with a different worldview never took offense to his Judeo-Christian stance because they saw genuine possibility in how he taught them. Evidence of lives changed and now willing to follow his God would come in the form of mail that was not sorted by pieces but weighed in bags.

If the number of years you live on earth is deemed successful when you write one book and deemed significant if you write two, how would you categorize one that wrote thirty? How would you pinpoint the moment when a struggling salesman authors a bestselling book on the Secrets of Closing the Sale or becomes a philosopher to be able to write another book that is just his views on selling? Great men are not born in extraordinary times. Great men redefine the time they live to be deemed extraordinary because they lived. Discipline is the hallmark of his appeal. He rises early to pray and then to write. Then he travels to speak and inspire. Then he returns to seek out the four generations of family so he can bless them.

Along the way he gives instruction of living and reminders of the gratitude we need to have for the nation we call home. He pauses to pull up the ones that sound different and look different. Like the Good Samaritan, he rescues them and then pays for their restoration. He then pays for their future lessons. I know--he showed me the love of God and demonstrated it through the love of man. When I asked him if I could borrow a book he referenced, he said no. His reasoning was simple. He liked to mark in them and was sure that I would forget to return it. You don't call someone a hero by their actions. You call them one because of what their actions lead to. I became fortunate in the next two decades to have a personal copy of most books he read on my desk for my own education. He had bought one for me as well. Thank you, Good Samaritan.

Throughout the annals of American history, from the midnight ride of Paul Revere until the Declaration of Independence, and from the Bay of Pigs until Ronald Reagan, we have seen unique people endowed with a special divine gift readied for human consumption. Some have answered the call and others went down in infamy because their ideas were wrong. George Orwell predicted that by 1984 we would have totalitarianism where freedom would become slavery, ignorance strength, and war would be considered peace. God can ask for sacrifice like He did with Abraham, a change in destination like He instructed to Jonah, or blind obedience as He mandated from Noah. Zig Ziglar met all three crossroads on a July 4th weekend when an enthusiastic lady named Sister Jessie led him to the saving grace of Jesus Christ. This champion of free enterprise, dubbed by his own peers as a salesman's salesman, was enjoying the success of a best-selling book called See You at the Top when obedience, destination, and message coalesced with clarity. He would have to sell America on herself while using a biblical framework to a secular audience who were on the heels of their own rebellion as flower children with bad music and worse hair. He would answer the call and unleash moral clarity that would get him recognized in the Halls of Congress. Statesmen would know his name. Entertainers, industrialists, businessmen, moguls, teachers, and civil servants would all flock to the seminars. The organization that would bear his name would now start training and facilitating seminars globally. American exceptionalism would be canvassed with Biblical values in business settings and prove that God's Word does not return void. The proverbial divide between secular and sacred would forever be conquered by one man who believed God had a plan for America and was not afraid to say so.

Adrian Rogers, an erudite preacher from Tennessee and a contemporary of Zig Ziglar, often said that failure was succeeding at the wrong things. Zig Ziglar would remind the world that failure was an event and could never be a person. These words and phrases resonated with the grandchildren of the grandfathers first impacted by Ziglar in the early '70s. A new generation of followers started practicing the principles and living out the values that had God, Family and Country as the cornerstone. When the image of a nation was being tarnished by ideological enemies abroad and the press in his own country, Zig Ziglar was more determined than ever to tout the values of America. He became a modern-day Webster and Henry, all packaged into one convincing voice. He would create imaginary tours of America in his talks and introduce us to people from all walks of life who were living the dream. We would meet the lady who escaped communism in Hungary to become successful in real estate in Michigan. We would encounter the blind car salesperson from Florida and the hot dog tycoon in California. Stories of heroism and real life Horatio Alger stories. Stories were his arrow and they hit the bull's eye with precision every time. How could you not identify with the overweight nurse from one seminar who specialized in bariatrics and became a doctor of eminence in another seminar? How can you not sympathize with a depressed housewife who then became one of the biggest sponsors of his events? God's salesman was just getting warmed up when most his age were considering retirement.

It is never the unknown that creates consternation. Sometimes it's the rote of things we do over and over that causes a mishap or two. One day at the top of the stairway a slip, a cry, a stop. The doctors think there is swelling on the brain. Physiotherapy begins. A life lived at a certain pace is slowed. The urgency of the moment intensifies as he becomes more resolute to finish well. He decides to write with clarity and purpose. Embrace the Struggle chronicles this season of life. His messages become more pungent as they reek of the goodness of God. When word spreads about his injury his CDs on faith and family start to fly off the shelves. People are encouraged at a healthier pace, not because they needed the Good News or that they were bad people. Like in any fight you root for the champion. They wanted to give the champion his due. The lines to greet him got longer as the collective conscience of a nation began to realize that this go-around might be the last one. He defied the odds for longer than expected. He stayed in the limelight, encouraging the lost to find hope in a Savior. He was going through the season of being stranded, shipwrecked, and imprisoned, and yet, like the Apostle Paul, kept on with the business of being diligent.

Thanksgiving is a holiday celebrated to remind ourselves of the gracefulness the early pilgrims had in a new frontier. Modernity has added the rituals of food, sports, and early shopping to get the best bargain on Christmas guilt. Thanksgiving has become many things, and somewhere in that mass of indulgence we all pause to give thanks. Thanks for what has happened. Thanks for what is about to happen, and prayerful thanks with one eye open for the food that is going to be consumed. Suddenly you receive a text message from the son that the father is hospitalized. You are asked to come because you knew him and he knew you. You drive to the hospital. You see him. You love him. You begin to wonder what your life would have been if he were never in it. Fear creeps over you but all you see is a family assured. All poised. He was the patriarch. The rock that inspired everyone. He was Zig Ziglar.

Then the words to a nation by the son a couple of days later that Zig Ziglar had gone home to be with the Lord. As he said many a' time, when (not if) he got to heaven he would run and find his mama and then go hug his baby girl. There was a reunion as America lost one of its legends, but heaven welcomed one of its heroes. Well done. The media picks up the story and the Internet is flying with reports, tributes, and I-remember-when stories. The tribute to honor his life was scripted by him and the songs sung to remember his legacy were chosen by him. He had orchestrated the finite details of his own memorial service in a letter to his pastor. Always determined, and yet ever compassionate, he appears on the video one last time and asks people to make a commitment to the Lord Jesus Christ. His reason is he wanted to be the first person to greet them in eternity. You can sell hope if you are hopeful. You can sell products and services if you are truthful.

You can only sell eternity if you believe it. Mr. Ziglar believed it. The sales program that was his life was now over. All the orders had been turned in. Heaven was tabulating the results of the contest. The winner was humanity. We won because God sent his salesperson to earth to ensure that His name would forever be glorified. America won because she claimed him on her team.

Thank you Mr. Z. Well Done......

LEGEND

6
MOE BERG

VOICED BY:
TREY GREEN

The legend of Moe Berg is told by my son, Trey Green.

Trey earned his Bachelor's in Economics from Liberty University at just Seventeen years old. He is currently working on his Master of Public Service and Administration with a concentration in Security Policy and Management at the Bush School of Government & Public Service at Texas A&M University.

Trey discovered this obscure hero several years ago through his baseball coach, Greg Edwards; who also happens to be our printer. Knowing we were a baseball family that loves to chase historical American legends, perhaps Greg shared the story of Berg with us in the hopes we would end up writing a book about it and sending him more print business. Well, he was right!

Moe Berg is a legend of liberty who, at great personal risk on many occasions, served as one of the most important spies in American history; significantly impacting WWII on several occasions. But this is not a man to whom one can apply only one "label." His intelligence gathering was greatly aided by the fact he was also a professional baseball player and a scholar who spoke more than a half dozen languages. Trey has correctly named him, The Renaissance Spy.

Like most spy stories, one finds it difficult to separate fact from fiction and myth. Reliable records of such exploits are purposefully destroyed, or never made in the first place. What we know for certain is that Moe Berg's actions earned him the Medal of Freedom from President Harry Truman in 1945; and Berg's baseball card is proudly displayed by the CIA at their headquarters in Langley, Virginia.

- Rick Green

Moe Berg
The Renaissance Spy

On April 18th, 1942, the United States launched 16 North American B-25 Mitchell bombers from the deck of the USS Hornet aircraft carrier. This entourage of American bombers, later known as "Doolittle's Raiders," was led by the famous Lieutenant Colonel Jimmy Doolittle. Their mission, regarded by many as a suicide run, was to strike a strategic psychological blow against Japan in response to the ruthless attacks on Pearl Harbor just a few months earlier. This mission was to be accomplished by each B-25 bomber dropping 2,000 pounds of explosives onto important Japanese military installations, factories, and other pieces of infrastructure in and around the city of Tokyo. Each of these targets were vital to Japan's future war effort, and would aid in slowing down their military progression.

In addition to the physical and psychological damage inflicted on the nation of Japan, the mission of Col. Doolittle and his Raiders involved something far more important to the war effort. It was their mission, their purpose, to give hope and passion back to the American people after the crushing events at Pearl Harbor.

On December 7th, 1941, in a move that shocked the American people, the nation of Japan sent a devastating aerial attack against a United States naval base stationed in Pearl Harbor. For many Americans, this attack shattered their sense of stability, security, and trust in the power of the United States' military. The political and military leaders of the United States knew that action needed to be taken quickly if hope and trust were to be restored in the hearts and minds of the American people.

Their answer to this crisis relied on the success of Col. Doolittle and his Raiders.

These men held the key to future success in the war effort in the palm of their hands; relying on the effectiveness of their skills and their willingness to take the fight to the very heart of the enemy Japanese nation to carry the day.

By God's grace, Col. Doolittle and his Raiders succeeded; igniting the passion of the American people once again and leading the United States to one of the most dedicated war efforts the world has ever seen. It was this passion that led the United States to take the fight deep within the heart of the Axis nations, pushing them back, and literally saving millions of lives.

Years after the war ended and peace was somewhat reestablished, questions and inquires began to arise as to the details of Doolittle's critical raid on Japan. The American people were curious as to how Col. Doolittle and other United States' military leaders were able to plan such an attack in only a few months; especially when the acquisition of intelligence on other nations usually takes a period of years, sometimes even decades. How was it then, that in only a few months, the United States was able to efficiently plan and coordinate one of the most successful and strategic attacks of the entire war effort? How was it that the United States was able to get specific and reliable intelligence on a hostile nation, to the point where each of Doolittle's bomber pilots knew the exact building that he was tasked with targeting, and exactly where that building was located?

The answer to this question, and the secret weapon behind the success of Doolittle's raid is a man named Moe Berg; a mysterious and eccentric major league baseball catcher.

————————————

Moe Berg was born on March 2nd, 1902, in New York, New York to Jewish parents. An intuitive, athletic, and ambitious child, Berg was three and a half years old when he started begging his mother to let him start school; and was seven years old when he discovered his love of baseball. His love for both academics and baseball grew, and Berg graduated as an honor student from Princeton University, where he also held a starting position on the baseball team for three years.

Berg received a degree in modern languages and was fluent in seven at the time of his graduation. After graduating from Princeton, Berg signed a contract with the Brooklyn Robins, successfully attaining his life long dream of playing major league baseball. Still wishing to develop his intellect on the side, Berg began attending law school at Columbia University just a few years later, placating his unquenchable thirst for knowledge for the time being.

Berg experienced many changes throughout his baseball career, moving between both positions and teams. Using his natural intelligence to his advantage, Berg studied every aspect the game of baseball and was often described by his teammates as the brainiest player in the major leagues. While Berg knew the game of baseball better than nearly anyone, he was never more than a mediocre player throughout this career. Strong on defense behind the plate, but with a weak offensive bat, Berg was never considered to be a top tier player.

Because he was never a star player, many people were surprised when Moe Berg was selected to join an American all star team for a series of games in the country of Japan. This team, composed of baseball legends like Babe Ruth, Lefty Gomez, and Lou Gehrig, consisted of the best that American baseball had to offer. The sheer amount of talent on this all star team caused many to question why Moe Berg, a third string catcher, was chosen to join this legendary entourage. The mystery of Berg's spot on the team confused many, with only a few knowing the truth, only a few knowing Berg's secret.

Moe Berg was a United States spy.

———————————

Prior to his being chosen for the all-star team, Moe Berg was recruited by the United States to take footage of various overseas locations for the purpose of intelligence gathering. Upon arriving in Japan, Berg made public appearances to establish his cover, even going so far as to address Japan's legislature for the purpose of strengthening political relations with the United States. Even though he was viewed as a public figure, when his team was off playing the Japan all star team, Berg often disappeared from the team without notice-and used his time to gather intelligence for the country that he so deeply loved.

On November 29th, 1934, the United States all star team faced off against the best of the Japanese baseball players in the city of Omiya. While this game was taking place, Moe Berg decided to leave, don a disguise, and sneak past security at the local Saint Luke's Hospital in Tokyo. Climbing the stairs to the top of the hospital building, Berg took out his camera and filmed various factories, military installations, and any other piece of infrastructure that he thought would be of interest to the United States intelligence community. Calmly, Berg then put away his camera and confidently exited the building, sneaking his camera and film past the security as he left. As Berg and the team toured Japan, they were searched multiple times by Japanese police and military personnel, yet the secret film was never once detected.

Even after his touring with the all star team was finished, Berg continued traveling through multiple countries, such as Russia, Korea, and even Poland. He filmed many critical locations in each of these areas, and often had his valuable film confiscated by the local police in each area. While Berg hated to lose intelligence on each of these countries, he steadfastly knew that the footage he took of Tokyo remained the most valuable, and must be protected with his life. Thankfully, Berg was able to keep this footage safe through the remainder of his travels, eventually arriving in the United States and screening the footage for the US military.

While Berg understood that his footage was vital, he could not have predicted just how important it would prove to be. When Lieutenant Colonel Jimmy Doolittle began to plan his famous raid, he found that an astonishing lack of precise intelligence existed on the layout of Tokyo buildings. Berg's intelligence, being the main source of information, proved to be one of the critical reasons behind the success of Doolittle's raid. The importance of Berg's contribution to Doolittle's success can not be overstated. Without Berg's intelligence, the war could have taken a dramatically different turn during the beginning years, and possibly ended with a different outcome as well.

————————————

Berg's feats and accomplishments on behalf of the United States do not end with his critical Tokyo mission, instead they continue for many years and in many different countries. After WWII began for the United States with the bombing of Pearl Harbor, Berg took up a position with Nelson Rockefeller's Office of the Coordinator of Inter-American Affairs; conducting various inspection services at military installations for nearly a year. In 1943, he joined the Office of Strategic Services' (OSS) Strategic Operations (SO) branch, where he would remain for the remainder of his intelligence career. In his capacity as a field agent, Berg was assigned to many different positions, such as the Secret Intelligence (SI) branch. While the OSS was certainly not known for their ingenious naming of departments and agencies, the work which they completed was essential to the war effort and the institution of peace after the conclusion of WWII.

Throughout his career, Berg experienced many secretive intelligence situations and missions worthy of a high budget Hollywood movie. During WWII, the country of Yugoslavia was occupied by the Nazi regime, with harsh actions being taken against the citizens of Yugoslavia. Resistance to the Nazis was strong within the nation as multiple groups sprung up and began to fight back. The United States, desiring to help these freedom fighters, needed to send someone into the occupied sections of Yugoslavia in order to determine which group to support and aid. The man they chose for this mission was Berg, and he willingly accepted. Parachuting into the middle of occupied territory, Berg met with both Draza Mihailovic and Josip Tito, two of the most famous WWII resistance fighters, in order to decide who the United States should support. Representing the US, Berg met with each leader, discussing their strategies, and ultimately decided that Josip Tito led the stronger and more efficient group; even though the US had mainly been supporting Mihailovic up until that time. Berg's evaluations were then used by the United States to determine how much support each group should receive, and which group should be given support first. Not even hesitating to parachute into hostile territory, Moe Berg gathered intelligence from groups who not only were in hiding, but were being actively hunted by the Nazis; a life threatening activity which Moe Berg was willing to face in order to aid the war effort.

After returning from his mission in Yugoslavia, Berg was assigned to Project AZUSA, where his goal was to meet Italian physicists and find out what they knew about the workings of particular German physicists. Continuing on to a similar mission, Berg was tasked with attending a lecture given by leading German physicist Werner Heisenberg. Heisenberg, considered to be an expert in the field of atomic research, was critical to any German advancement towards weapons of mass destruction. Berg was instructed to attend the lecture and ascertain whether the Germans were close to obtaining an atomic bomb. If Berg believed that the Germans were close, he had orders to present his firearm and kill Heisenberg on the spot; making his assignment a suicide mission. Even with the knowledge that mission would require him to sacrifice his own life, Berg willingly accepted and flew to Zurich to attend the lecture.

Thankfully, Berg concluded that nothing Heisenberg said alluded to the Germans being close to the creation of an atomic bomb. Because of this, after Berg listened and talked personally to Heisenberg, he walked away from the lecture without the need to sacrifice his life, allowing him to further serve the United States.

Moe Berg's missions and investigations were completed in the shadows, without recognition. Berg, so used to the fame that comes with major league sports and the traveling with an all star team, used his intellectual skills to enter the private and quiet world of espionage and risk his life for his country. The dangerous situations he encountered, combined with the actions that he himself took, led to a life of near death experiences that most would never consider pursuing.

After a life of such peril and sacrifice, Berg retired from government service in the year 1954 to a life of eccentricity and obscurity with his family. Prior to his retirement, Berg was awarded one of the highest civilian awards, the Medal of Freedom, to honor his actions and dedication to the United States. Due to the attention that it would surely bring upon him, attention that he felt he did not deserve, Moe Berg turned down the Medal of Freedom just a couple of months after it was awarded to him. Years later, after his death, it was accepted by his sister; giving Berg the formal recognition for his feats that he so aptly deserved. Prior to his death, Berg was involved in various business ventures, some successful and others failures; but for the most part lived out the remainder of his life in anonymity, without fame or fortune.

Unlike most legends, Berg is relatively unknown; even though his life was composed of game changing decisions and actions. His intelligence gathering and self sacrifice quite literally helped shape the Second World War as we now know it, yet Berg never received recognition for his feats during his lifetime. Instead, his sacrifice went unnoticed for the most part, something that Berg was content with. He did not serve the United States for the purposes of fame, he did so because he felt it was his duty. He did not care for recognition or fame, he was content with simply doing his duty for his country, then returning to his private life.

Berg's legend serves as a clarifier when it comes to identifying legends and heroes throughout history. Unlike most legends, Berg was not famous or well known. His work was conducted in the shadows, yet was just as effective as the work done by public and celebrated heroes. This type of legend is one which applies to many of us within society. To become effective for a cause, to advance a movement, to make a difference; does not always require your name to be in the lights. It does not require fame or recognition, it simply requires doing your duty. It requires dedication even when your actions go unnoticed, when your successes only occur behind the closed curtains, away from the press and cameras. This type of dedication, one which does not require fame to solidify an understanding of its importance; is the type of dedication that lies within many great legends and heroes.

Many of us, like Moe Berg, must keep in mind the true reason for our passion towards a cause within society. Our validation should not come through recognition, it should come through knowledge. It should come through knowledge of a job well done, of a cause and a purpose advanced, of a country defended. Our passion and validation should arrive through the knowledge that we have assisted in the advancement of something greater than ourselves, and that we do not require accompanying fame in order to appease our sense of duty.

Like Moe Berg, many of us must be willing to fight in the shadows and leave the flashing lights to someone else.

LEGEND 7

SYBIL
LUDINGTON

VOICED
BY:
KAMRYN
GREEN

The legend of Sybil Ludington is told by my daughter, Kamryn Green.

Kamryn began researching Sybil when we were filming *Chasing American Legends* (ChasingAmericanLegends.com). We had a chance to visit Sybil's hometown in Carmel, New York, and Kamryn spent time with biographer V.T. Dacquino. Kamryn was greatly moved by Sybil's story because of their shared age and love of liberty.

Kamryn writes the story of Sybil in the increasingly popular "faction" or "historical fiction" style. This style uses the known facts of the story, but inserts creative writing of what probably happened, or could have happened, and does not contradict known facts. For example, we do not know exactly what happened on Sybil's ride, or the exact conversation she had with her parents and the troops she mustered. So Kamryn gives us a version of the story as she believes it could have occurred, while holding true to the portions of the story we know actually happened.

We do not present this story as historical fact, but rather as a creative, fictional account based upon historical fact.

Sybil Ludington is a Legend of Liberty who exhibited extraordinary courage and skill for the cause of liberty.

- Rick Green

Accepting the Call

The rain feels like pelting bullets.

Thunder signals an even bigger storm is headed toward Carmel within the hour. It's been two hours since I left just after dusk into the clouded night, every ounce of determination inside me bubbling to the surface.

My father's instructions were clear. Ride as fast as I can to each of the homes of his minutemen. Being a girl may have kept me from being an official member of the militia, but I've been at almost every drill, grown up with their kids, had dinner in their homes. I know where to go and who to find. Father said to beat on the door of every patriot soldier and yell with purpose.

Warn the people. Rally the men.

My only companion is my trusted steed. I've explored these trails and woods with Star so many times, we gallop as one through every twist and turn.

But this storm is worse than any we have faced. She lets out a snort of dissatisfaction as we dodge rampant limbs. Winds become stronger. I grab my drenched skirt and bundle it up in my fist, and we trample through the saturated ground. My eyes avert from the trail to the house ahead on my right, no lights from inside, no sign of life anywhere on the property.

But I know this is the home of a man I've seen in father's militia, so I cannot pass it by.

I raise the stick in my worn out hand and grip the reins with the other.

"To Arms! To Arms! The British are coming! The British are coming!" Drops of rain slide down my cracked lips as the shouts tear from my lungs. I don't even bother to hop off Star as I beat on the wooden door three times. "Meet the Colonel at his house immediately! The British Troops are burning Danbury!" I start to gallop away in search of the next house when a man appears from inside the cabin.

"What's all this noise in the middle of the night? Who are you?"

"Sir, it's me, Sybil, the colonel's daughter." His face shows sudden recognition of my drenched figure. "I was sent to inform you of British troops burning Danbury. We need as many men as possible! The Colonel requests you and your arms immediately."

Thunder continues to roar, making it difficult to be heard over the storm.

But the man has already heard enough. He's back inside and I can hear him throwing his gear together and waking his family. My heart aches as I imagine the fear he is watching swell up in his family's eyes.

I turn Star around to face the woods when the door to the average sized cabin swings open once again.

"Wait! Sybil!" The man guards his eyes from the drenching rain as his cloaks and garments become more soaked by the minute. "How long have you been riding in this horrible weather? You cannot continue by yourself with so many dangers are out there!"

I blink away my watery vision. "I left at dusk, sir. I am aware of the dangers I may encounter, but we all have to make sacrifices for our freedom, and this is what I've been called to do."

"Yes, you are a very brave girl, but what about your father? They're looking for him, they'll be looking for you!"

I nod firmly. "I am aware—"

"Skinners occupy these woods Sybil." The man squints his eyes in the rain, raising his hand to gesture to the dark and cold woods behind me.

I pause, glancing down. Breathing in, I fight a shiver from the bitter air. "Yes, I am also aware of the Cowboys and Skinners that these woods harbor." I look up and lock with the man's eyes, resolve in my voice. "But I am ready. I mean no disrespect, but I cannot waste another moment sitting around. You and I have been called to arms!"

I search the man's eyes one last time, knowing that this could be the last that I see of this fellow soldier and friend. A chill travels across my bare skin, but not from the cold. I know what's out there; I've explored every trail and crevice alongside my father since I was a child. I've experienced threatening situations more than once in my life...but nothing like this.

With a slight nudge and a click of my tongue, Star bursts into a gallop and I charge the menacing woods head on with my chin tilted high. A strong force of wind whips my ponytail off my shoulder, causing me to huddle closer to my rugged cloak. A shiver runs down my spine as I think of my siblings huddled together in the cellar below our house; questions crowding their minds. I want to be there with them...I want to comfort them like I have in the past. I want to temper their big imaginations and assure them everything will be alright.

I want to so badly, but I can't this time. I have to believe in my ability to do this, to finish what I started. I squint my eyes and furrow my brow against the increasing rain. Something quiets my soul...something much deeper than any sensation of peace. No, it's not a false feeling of assurance that there will be warmth and shelter soon enough.

Because there won't be.

I can feel God's hand tapping my shoulder. He's telling me that it will be hard. It will be dreadful, painful, and people will suffer.

I will suffer.

But I know that He's telling me He will be there through it all. And it's not barely enough, but all I need to get through.

Adrenaline grows inside as I continue pushing on. We trudge through the caky ground and complex terrain. We never consider quitting, never stopping for more than a few seconds of rest.

My eyes are wide open and alert. My mind is speaking to the rest of my body with words of determination; reaching back to recall every bit of information that might help make this easier. I've grown up with the teachings of my father sown into my heart. Not just teachings of right and wrong, but those of the local militia and strategies on war. Knowing there is very little chance this will get any easier; I just have to keep going.

I know it's in my blood to finish this.

"Star, go! Agh!!!"

A tattered piece of my skirt is torn clean off by a pair of coarse hands. I see the moon reflect off of his eyes. A dark eagerness hidden behind them, like a wild animal drooling for its prey.

I cling to my saddle with everything I have and grip the stick in my right hand, knowing that my life depends on it.

"Come here you little brat!" Yellow teeth flash through a gritted smile.

He reaches and grasps for the stick in my hands. I pull back, jabbing it forward at the Skinner's throat. Once, twice, a third time with all my strength.

He fingers at his neck, face turning beat red with pain. But he doesn't stop persisting, clasping my ankle to drag me off Star, his soiled hands squeezing and pulling.

I grunt, sucking in a sharp breath, gripping the saddle even harder.

My hand fumbles with the stick, gripping it just strong

enough to thrust it again. My face contorts, and I hold nothing back, feeling the Skinner's throat give to the pressure of the stick damaging something underneath.

A gasp escapes his mouth as he starts to gag; releasing my ankle and scratching at his throat. Reaching high above my head, with one final swing of the stick, I strike the side of his head with every bit of strength I have left. He stumbles around like a drunkard, struggling to regain composer.

My mind orders me to move immediately.

"Run Star! Go!"

Throwing myself at Star's neck and digging my ankles into her side, we storm away, leaving the huffing figure on the stiff ground behind us.

I pant uncontrollably, thoughts running wild in my head. Quickly glancing back to make sure the Skinner is staying on the ground where he belongs, I plunge ahead with Star into the woods once again.

Exhausted wheezing comes out of me and a pounding ache starts to pulse in my temples. Allowing the rain to bathe my skin, I carefully bend down towards my ankle and rub it where the uncontrollable stranger grabbed and pulled.

My body is begging for rest, as I wonder how much longer I'll have to endure the aches and bitter taste of the freezing night. With weariness, my eyelids begin to droop, and a whisper slides off my lips. "Why must it be like this..."

I think of the those whose pain far exceeds mine. A knowing pain that must lye in every brave hearted solider...choosing to leave his doorstep, knowing of the fear buried inside his loved ones as he goes off to battle.

I rub Star's neck, tempted to bury my face in her matted mane where I may find a little bit of warmth. I don't know what I'm asking for, or what I want anymore. I just know the way it is right here, right now, and what I'm supposed to do about it. What I've been called to do about it.

Keep going.

So I squeeze my legs and prod Star a little bit more; wary of slowing at all for fear of another bandit surprising me from the darkness like the Skinner who nearly had me.

Never stopping, even as daunting thoughts and assumptions linger in the back of my head. Memories of my home and the faces of my family flash through my mind.

I remember the feeling that was building inside me just a few hours ago when the scout frantically hastened to our door with tonight's warning. I was uneasy at the sight of my panicked mother and terrified siblings. Short of breath, the rider explained the attacks on Danbury and the marching of the British.

The scene from earlier tonight is crystal clear as I re-live every moment in my mind. Those moments that might have been the last I ever spent with the ones I love most.

Earlier that evening, around dusk...

The lanterns around our house flicker as the moon makes its first appearance of the night and darkness begins to descend.

Fog drapes the ground around our property as voices in the house get louder and louder. The enemy has already burned most of Danbury, Connecticut and we are likely next.

"What do you plan on doing?" The alarm lingers in my mother's voice.

Father paces the floor with anticipation in each step, rubbing his hand up and down his beard in deep thought. "Someone has to muster my regiment, I need to be here to give orders. I—I need someone to ride, to wake them up."

We exchange whispers for a few minutes and try to figure out a solution, any solution to get us through. I cringe at the agitation in their voices as my attention is drawn to movement outside our window. It's now dark and precious minutes are ticking by. Heavy rains begin pouring over Carmel, all the way to Kent Cliffs. My eyes begin darting back and forth from my parents to the window when I hear my name.

"Sybil. Sybil, I know you can do it."

Me? He wants me to muster the troops?

My eyes wonder around the room as I ponder what is being asked of me. Not just for this night, but for the days and years that lie ahead. What will I have to do...what am I being called to give up?

The enemy is burning everything in their path, thirsty for the blood of their foes, and I have just been called to awaken those in my own backyard to fight back. I've always thought it would be others doing the dangerous things, the midnight rides and the musket battles.

But now I know. I, too, must stand and fight. I must face danger as well.

A crack of lightning outside grabs my attention and I wonder how hard the late night ride will be in the storms. My mind tries to calculate the risk of riding in this storm through very difficult terrain; clouds preventing much help from the moon to light the way. And then, there are the Skinners and Cowboys that inhabit these woods and hate my father.

Can I do this?

Does Father really believe I can?

Do I believe I can?

"Henry, our own daughter?" I glance at my mother with a furrowed brow as she leans in closer to my father's figure. For a moment, her concern weakens my resolve. But I shake the doubts quickly.

I know I am ready.

I've trained my whole life for such a time as this.

"Father," I say with all the confidence and finality I can muster, my face and posture indicating the discussion is over, the decision is made.

"Where do you need me to go?"

It was April 26, 1777 when Sybil completed her mission. She finished the job. She answered the call.

Riding 40 miles through the rain and mud, she woke every

armed patriot she could reach. They, in turn, warned others and by late morning, approximately 500 men were armed and ready to charge against the enemy.

Place yourself in Sybil's shoes. Imagine hearing not only the call of your earthly Father, but a sense of Divine destiny from your heavenly Father.

First, it should be noted that Sybil was a very smart young lady. She was not unprepared on that grueling night. This sixteen-year-old trained regularly to become a great rider. She paid attention and learned about the strategies her father used when leading his men into battle. She learned early in life the importance of protecting her family when trouble threatened to knock on their door and there was no one else around to do the job.

By the time she accepted the call to arms, she was already trained as well, if not better, than the average messenger or spy.

This young woman knew what she was doing.

Yet, she was still just sixteen years old. That's only one year older than me! But the courage and maturity that she had was more than enough to accomplish the task at hand. I am sure that fear of the future was in the back of her mind, but she never let that stop her. If I were in her shoes, the thought of riding into the dead of the night with only a horse and a stick, knowing there are British troops getting closer every minute, would seem sort of... well... terrifying, to say the least! As if that were not enough, being the eldest daughter of the chief

LIFE LESSONS

law enforcement officer in the area, she was a prime target of the bandits.

The enemy was out to capture or kill anyone from the other side that came across their paths. Including Sybil Ludington.

So, what can we learn from Sybil? Go back in time and imagine yourself in her shoes. Picture the flicker of the lanterns, the fear on your mother's face, the determination in your father's eyes. Feel the struggle between your own fears and your desire to contribute to the cause.

What will you do?

Will you ignore what is being asked of you and simply state that the job is too hard?

That would have been the easy thing for Sybil to do. No one expected a woman to accept this task, especially at her age. She could have simply told her father she was not ready to ride into the thick of the night for nine or more hours.

But she did not take the easy way out. She accepted the challenge.

Could you face such a challenge head on and trust in the power of God to help you get through it?

Often, we get so caught up in the craziness of life and want to take the easy route, avoiding the more challenging paths along which there is greater reward and results. We may not be asked to make a dangerous midnight ride or fight on the front lines of a war. But each of us are called to serve in one way or another, to fulfill the purpose that God placed within our heart.

Sybil has been such an inspiration to me because of her bravery to do something that was far above expectations for a young female in that day. She had no way of knowing how that night would end. But she knew what she was doing could protect her family and their freedom.

Trudging through the rain and mud during a bitter night with the cries of battle lurking close by, Sybil Ludington most definitely did not take the easy route.

Sadly, so many people in this generation do.

They sit back and watch the fight happen, oblivious to the fact that their own freedoms, and the ones belonging to those around them, are being stolen right from their fingertips.

They trick themselves into thinking that the battle will never happen in their community or their back yard.

Here's the truth of the matter...the battles for freedom are not just with other countries.

Pain, war, and confrontation can show up at your doorstep and in your neighborhood with very little, if any, warning.

What if you aren't prepared to fight?

I challenge you. No matter where you are or what you are doing, take a moment to think about the serious trouble that our country is in today. And then ask yourself what you're going to do about it.

Yes, you...

Are you just going to sit idly by and ignore the responsibility that has been passed down to you? Or like so many legends of liberty that truly understood what it means to protect and preserve freedom, will you use your voice, use your one life you have to give, and accept the call to defend freedom?

Perhaps your call is to help educate others, or train to physically fight against evil, or run for political office, or raise your children to be future legends of liberty. Whatever specific call of duty is placed on your life, think of Sybil and be as courageous as her.

My prayer and dream for this nation is that we would recognize the challenges before us and then charge them head on with every ounce of our being, never hesitating to use that voice and one life.

Join me in this fight.

Pick up you arms. Whether horse and stick, pen and paper, or whatever the tools of your calling.

Be a Sybil Ludington of today.

Patriot and soldier, defender of liberty and preserver of the torch, gather your courage and accept the call to arms.

For you have been called for such a time as this.

Let's do this thing!

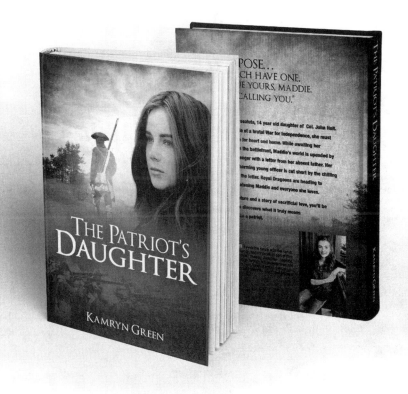

Check out Kamryn Green's stand alone novel, The Patriot's Daughter.

Loaded with adventure and a story of sacrificial love, you'll be inspired as Maddie Holt discovers what it truly means to fight and love like a patriot.

Visit RickGreen.com/KamsKorner for more information.

LEGEND 8

GEORGE WASHINGTON

VOICED BY:

TIM BARTON

The legend of George Washington being bulletproof is told by Tim Barton.

Tim is a speaker, author, and radio host, traveling the nation speaking and training on the founding principles of America. He has a true gift for teaching young people and instilling in them a passion for truth, despite the culture around them tearing down any concept of moral absolutes.

Tim and his wife, Gabi, are a part of our leadership team training students at Patriot Academy to lead their generation out of this cultural darkness and rebuild the foundations of a strong society.

You can learn more about Tim and book him for your local event by visiting WallBuilders.com.

George Washington could have been a part of this first volume of Legends of Liberty for many, many reasons. The specific legend of his being "bulletproof" is the subject of Tim's chapter because this particular story played such a critical role in the nation's perception of George Washington and, indeed, his own perception of himself and the calling God had on his life.

You can read an even more in-depth version of this legend in David Barton's, *The Bulletproof George Washington*, and even listen to an audio version narrated by Dean Jones. Both are available at WallBuilders.com.

This story is also the subject of a *Chasing American Legends* episode, Bulletproof President?, available at ChasingAmericanLegends.com.

- Rick Green

Bulletproof Washington

In the mid-1700s, before America was a nation, the French and British fought for control of the land in the interior parts of America, eastward of the Mississippi River, in what was known as the French and Indian War. In this war, the Indians primarily joined sides with the French, while the Americans sided with the British.

In February 1755, British General Edward Braddock arrived from England with two full regiments to oppose the French soldiers. This was the first time a substantial body of British troops had arrived in America. General Braddock's job was to expel the French forces and reclaim the Ohio Valley territory.

Upon his arrival in America, General Braddock heard tales of a young American officer whom he sought to add to his staff. The sought after young Colonel was Twenty-three-year-old George Washington.

Even though George Washington was a young man, he had already made a name for himself as a courageous and heroic individual. At the age of Twenty-one, he had been dispatched to carry an appeal to the French General St. Pierre. The commander of French forces stationed at Fort

Erie in northwestern Pennsylvania was to be asked to respect the English claim to the Ohio Valley territory. It was a Five-Hundred-mile journey through a pathless wilderness and it took George nearly six weeks to reach Fort Erie. This journey proved to be a fruitless effort as the French General refused to receive the English appeal. General St. Pierre told Washington that his orders required him to oust every Englishman from the Ohio Valley and he meant to carry out those orders to the letter. Washington was told that France claimed the area and she intended to make good on her claim by force of arms, if necessary.

When Washington began his return to Virginia with the French reply, it was the dead of winter. On his journey home, he and his guide, Christopher Gist, were ambushed by Indians. They were able to escape the initial attack and fled all that night and through the next day. Upon reaching a large river, they were disheartened to see that the river had begun freezing but had not completely frozen over. This meant they would not be able to walk across on a frozen path and would instead have to build a raft.

They worked diligently throughout that day to make a raft and shortly after sunset, the raft was complete. George and Christopher climbed on the raft and began to navigate the icy, fast flowing waters. Their raft quickly lodged into an ice jam and the fast moving waters threatened to sink the raft. George pushed his pole in the water trying to unjam the raft but his pole was swept away and he was pulled into the freezing water. He was able to grasp onto one of the logs on the raft and save his own life.

Despite their tireless efforts, George and Christopher were unable to direct the raft to the other side of the river. As the raft continued with the current, the two men were able to get the raft to an island in the middle of the river. On that island, they endured a cold, wet, freezing and miserable night. The next morning, the river had frozen over and they were able to walk across to the other side.

They made the return trip to Virginia in only four weeks. During the entire ten-week journey to and from the French fort, Washington kept a journal. Upon returning to Williamsburg, Virginia, the Maryland Gazette (a popular newspaper) published his account. Word quickly spread throughout the colonies of Washington's bravery and persistence that allowed him to overcome such incredible odds.

In spite of his best efforts, Washington's negotiations with the French had failed and now the conflict would be resolved through war. During negotiations, Washington had seen much of the French preparations at Fort Erie and he was commissioned to lead a group of men to capture a strategic position on the river to prevent the French from advancing. On the way, some sixty miles south of their intended target, Washington learned from his Indian scouts that the French were marching toward his group. Washington had his men quickly erect a small stockade in the middle of a field. This stockade, very appropriately, became known as Fort Necessity.

Washington's entire force numbered around three hundred, and while he had been awaiting reinforcements, the French and her allies had been gathering in much larger numbers, strengthening their position. Washington patiently waited over the next month for reinforcements, but deciding he could wait no longer, he set out to dislodge the enemy.

After advancing only thirteen miles, his scouts reported that French General De Villiers was approaching with a massive army of French and Indians. Realizing the military impossibility of his situation, Washington fell back to Fort Necessity to save his soldiers. His forces had scarcely secured the little fort when De Villiers and his 1,100 men arrived and surrounded them. The French stationed themselves on the tops of the knolls looking down into the fort, and many of the Indians climbed into the treetops where, concealed by thick foliage, they fired down into the fort upon the exposed Americans. For nine long hours, a continuous shower of musket balls was poured in upon them.

The Americans returned the fire of the French with unabated vigor, but Washington's men were steadily being killed. Washington – greatly outnumbered, unreinforced, and without sufficient food and supplies – knew it would be impossible to hold out much longer; so when De Villiers proposed that the Americans surrender, Washington accepted the honorable terms of surrender offered him. On July 4th, 1754, his little army (which had been allowed to keep its remaining equipment and provisions) marched out of the tiny fort they had so courageously defended, and returned to Virginia.

Washington's fame and the stories of his heroism again spread throughout the colonies. Soon thereafter, Virginia's Governor Dinwiddie reorganized the militia and permitted no rank higher than captain; this meant that George Washington could no longer be a Colonel. Upon his demotion, Washington resigned to return to his family's farm. However, when General

Braddock arrived in America, he heard numerous accounts of young Washington and invited Washington to join his staff with his previous rank of Colonel.

Washington was excited to be back in action and he was thankful for the opportunity to learn and study under such a renowned professional soldier as General Braddock.

Before Washington accepted the invitation to join General Braddock, his mother, Mary, rode to meet him at Mount Vernon. She discouraged George from joining Braddock's staff, fearing he would be in too great a danger, but George had already experienced God's protection in his life and was convinced this same Divine protection would remain with him. He explained to her:

His mother yielded and pledged her continued prayer, promising him:

> *"The God to whom you commended me, madam, when I set out upon a more perilous errand, defended me from all harm, and I trust He will do so now. Do you not?"* [1]

George Washington and 100 Virginia Buckskins joined Braddock's soldiers.

> *"That God may protect you through all the dangers and hardships of war and return you in safety will be my constant prayer. With His blessing you can be a useful man in war as in peace, and without it you can expect nothing."* [2]

In May 1755, General Braddock and his troops marched

toward the French Fort Duquesne (near what is now Pittsburgh, PA). Their troop was so large that the line of marching soldiers was over 4 miles long!

After weeks of marching, and when they were only a few miles from the French Fort Duquesne, General Braddock unknowingly led his troops into a waiting ambush. The French and Indians, who were hiding in the woods, opened fire on the British troops. Even though the British had a much larger army, General Braddock was unaccustomed to fighting an enemy that would not face him on an open field. Although thoroughly skilled in the tactics of European warfare, he mistakenly believed that battles could be fought in America as they had long been fought in Europe – that soldiers would march directly against their opponents on an open field of battle just as if both were on a military parade ground before an arena of spectators.

The French and Indians had no such compulsions.

The French and Indians, who had been hiding and waiting in ambush, slaughtered the British soldiers, who made easy targets in their bright red uniforms. The British were instantly overwhelmed and essentially trapped in the narrow road they had cut through the wilderness. The British troops could see powder smoke from the French and Indians muskets in the woods, but they were not able to see the men who were shooting at them. They began firing back aimlessly into the woods. Their bullets were having no effect.

The French and Indians continued to fire volley after volley to a devastating effect. The ground became littered with the dead and dying. The British ranks were in utter confusion. As more British troops died with each volley, the British soldiers became so panic-stricken that they were disoriented and immobile.

The Virginian soldiers (many of whom came with Washington) took the more practical approach and adopted the Indian style of fighting and found trees and rocks to hide behind. They did not fire aimlessly into the woods, but looked and waited until an adversary revealed an arm, head or exposed any part of themselves that could be a target. As the British soldiers saw the Virginians taking cover and firing from protected positions, they began to adopt this tactic.

General Braddock, however, thought this method a very cowardly way to fight and ordered his troops to stop hiding and protecting themselves behind rocks and trees, demanding they remain exposed on the field of battle. This allowed the slaughter to continue.

As the battle raged, the Indians specifically targeted the British and American officers. They knew that if they could kill the officers, the remaining troops would scatter. During the course of the battle, they shot EVERY mounted officer except ONE.

George Washington was the only mounted officer not shot down in that battle, but he did have two horses shot out from under him. After hours of a brutal slaughter, every officer except General Braddock and George Washington had been shot. The Indians continued targeting the two remaining officers, Braddock and Washington. General Braddock was finally shot and George Washington assumed control of the troops.

When the troops saw Braddock fall, there was utter chaos. They began to flee for their lives. Washington fought to regain control of the troops and led them in a retreat to safety.

As the British troops retreated, the French and Indians could have easily overtaken the frightened and fleeing men and completely wiped them out; but they were so surprised and elated by their victory, that the Indians raced toward the field where the slaughter had taken place and began to scalp and plunder the fallen soldiers. Because the British troops had fled in utter panic, they left all of their supplies on the field: the wagons, guns, artillery, cattle, horses, baggage and provisions. These supplies proved too tempting for the French and Indians to abandon to pursue the fleeing British.

It took the British many days to return to Fort Cumberland. The French and Indians, after their victory celebration, could have easily caught up with the fleeing troops but with the British army being so annihilated, the French decided they were no longer a viable threat and allowed the starving, wounded and scared British to struggle back to Virginia.

When George Washington and the surviving troops got back to Fort Cumberland, news had already spread of the massacre. Washington wrote his mother and brother a letter to assure them of his safety. He told them that, "...by the all-powerful dispensations of Providence I have been protected beyond all human probability or expectation; for I had four bullets through my coat and two horses shot under me yet escaped unhurt, although death was leveling companions on every side of me." [3]

Word of Washington's miraculous survival spread quickly. Both the Indians from the battle and the American colonists sang his praise. One Indian warrior explained, "Washington was never born to be killed by a bullet! For, I had seventeen fair fires at him with my rifle, and after all could not bring him to the ground!" [4] This seems a remarkable account considering that a skilled marksman rarely misses their mark, much less 17 times.

One Indian Chief, Red Hawk, who had been instrumental in the French victory, told of shooting eleven different times at Washington without hitting him; and because his gun had never before missed its mark, Red Hawk ceased firing at him, convinced that the Great Spirit protected Washington. [5]

15 years after this battle, in 1770, which was then a time of peace, Washington traveled with his friend to explore uninhabited regions near the same area where he had previously battled the French and Indians. A company of Indians came to their camp one night and a Chief stepped forward and, recalling the battle from 15 years earlier, told Washington, "I have traveled a long and weary path that I might see the young warrior of the great battle. It was on the day when the white man's blood mixed with the streams of our forest that I first beheld this chief [indicating Washington]. I called to my young men and said, "Quick! Let your aim be certain, and he dies." Our rifles were leveled – rifles which, but for you, knew not how to miss. 'Twas all in vain; a power mightier far than we shielded you. Seeing you were under the special guardianship of the Great Spirit, we immediately ceased to fire at you...The Great Spirit protects that man [again indicating Washington], and guides his destinies – he will become the chief of nations,

and a people yet unborn will hail him as the founder of a mighty empire. I am come to pay homage to the man who is the particular favorite of Heaven and who can never die in battle." [6]

This Indian Chief recognized God's hand of protection on George Washington, and history confirms that he was right. True to the chief's prediction, and because God sovereignly and Divinely protected him, Washington not only did not die in that 1755 battle, but he was not even wounded in that or in any of the numerous subsequent battles in which he fought.

There are numerous examples throughout the American Revolution where Washington could have and likely should have been gunned down, but God's protecting hand covered Washington. As a result of numerous Providential interventions throughout his life, Washington became – just as the old Indian chief had accurately prophesied – the chief of a nation and was hailed by subsequent generations as a founder – in fact, as the Father – of his country.

Among George Washington's many remarkable accomplishments, one that is worth noting is that at times, because of Divine intervention, he was bulletproof.

---

[1] Benson Lossing, *Mary and Martha: The Mother and the Wife of George Washington* (New York: Harper & Brothers, 1886), p. 49 (online: https://books.google.com/books?id=Cx4FAAAAYAAJ&pg=PA49#v=onepage&q&f=false).

[2] William Thayer, *Young People's Life of George Washington* (New York: John R. Anderson & Co., 1883), p. 199 (online: https://books.google.com/books?id=JVxjHoPvYt4C&pg=PA199#v=onepage&q&f=false).

[3] George Washington, *The Writings of George Washington*, Jared Sparks, editor (Boston: Russell, Odiorne, and Metcalf, 1834), Vol. II, p. 89, to John A. Washington on July 18, 1755.

[4] M. L. Weems, *The Life of George Washington* (Philadelphia: Joseph Allen, 1837), pp. 43-44 (online: https://books.google.com/books?id=6tc56rgYE1YC&pg=PA43#v=onepage&q&f=false).

[5] Samuel Kercheval, *A History of the Valley of Virginia* (Woodstock, VA: John Gatewood, 1850), p. 320 (online: https://books.google.com/books?id=dVQVAAAAYAAJ&pg=PA320#v=onepage&q&f=false).

[6] George Washington Parke Custis, *Recollections and Private Memoirs of Washington* (New York: Derby & Jackson, 1860), pp. 303-304 (online: https://books.google.com/books?id=PkE6AAAAcAAJ&pg=PA303#v=onepage&q&f=false).

LEGEND 9

BRIAN BIRDWELL

VOICED BY:

REAGAN GREEN

The legend of Brian Birdwell is told by my son, Reagan Green.

Reagan has looked up to Brian for many years. Brian has spoken at Patriot Academy many times, guest starred in a *Chasing American Legends* episode at Arlington Cemetery, and our family has enjoyed supporting Brian as a Texas State Senator.

I try to purposefully get my kids around men and women who exhibit strong leadership traits, while living out Biblical principles and Christian character. Brian Birdwell is certainly that kind of man and it is a priviledge to honor him with this chapter.

Brian Birdwell is a living Legend of Liberty for his service and sacrifice to America, the moral clarity with which he speaks and leads, and the investment he continues to make in the lives of so many others.

- Rick Green

Lieutenent Colonel Brian Birdwell

Perhaps more than any living American, Lt. Col. Brian Birdwell knows the fiery depths of terrorism in its worst form.

On September 11, 2001, the world as we knew it changed forever. That was the day America suffered the worst attack ever on her homeland in a single day. It was a hard blow from the tyranny of terrorism, and it tested the limits of America's courage, honor, and sacrifice.

On the morning of the attacks, Col. Birdwell began what he thought would be a normal day. Before his usual routine of scanning headlines, reading briefing reports, and reviewing his calendar, he started his day with God. He was working his way through Charles Stanley's, On Holy Ground. After his devotional time, he set out to work.

Birdwell worked at the Pentagon as a military assistant to the Deputy Assistant Chief of Staff for Installation Management (ACSIM). When he arrived at the office he greeted some co-workers and made small talk about things people talk about when the day is so uneventful. Little did they know that the biggest topic of the year, and many more to come, would soon occur right where they were greeting each other.

At around nine o'clock, a co-worker of Birdwell's, Sandi Taylor, received a phone call from her daughter telling her that the World Trade Center in New York City had been hit by a plane. Birdwell, Sandi, and another co-worker, Cheryle Sincock, rushed to the conference room and turned on the television. They tried to figure out what was going on, but all they could do was watch and take calls from other Pentagon spectators, asking "are you seeing this?" While watching, they witnessed the second airliner blast through the south tower sending fire and debris tumbling onto the street below. The second plane confirmed what everyone suspected—America was under attack.

They began debating who might be responsible for this attack when Sandi got another call from her daughter warning her to get out of the building because she was afraid that the Pentagon was also a target. Col. Birdwell dismissed the idea, insisting terrorists would never be so foolish as to attack the Pentagon and bring the entire U.S. military down on them. He then excused himself to use the restroom.

That was the last time he spoke to Cheryle and Sandi.

As Col. Birdwell exited the restroom and started back down the hall, the outside wall of the corridor exploded in a hailstorm of fire, throwing Col. Birdwell back, and deafening him. Everything around him went black, as if he was thrown into a deep, dark cave. A loud blast of fire exploded next to him, slamming him across the hall, tossing him limp onto the floor. He heard debris flying all around, ceiling panels and light fixtures were crashing down. He couldn't see anything except for a ring of yellow surrounding him.

He then realized...he was on fire!

The pain came instantly. The heat was so intense that the polyester pants of his uniform melted into his legs. His arms, back, legs, and hair were lit with flames. Thick smoke engulfed him, slapping him across the face and threatening to suffocate him. His mind registered a distant odor and taste.

Jet fuel?

As he struggled to breathe, he choked on heavy vapors and debris. The smoke and heat stung his eyes. He didn't know where the fire was coming from or where the explosion had happened. All he could see was the intense glow of yellow around him, and around that was total blackness. His body screamed in pain, but there was nothing to put out the flames. He forced his eyes open and tried to get to his feet, but his body would not cooperate. In order to survive whatever this was, he knew he had to escape... and fast.

Disoriented from the blast, smoke, and fire, he couldn't tell which way was safe and which was danger. He just knew he had to get out. He had to get somewhere else. He tried several times to escape, but his body could not hold him, he had no balance, and was in so much pain.

He was fading quickly.

Finally, he knew he couldn't get out, and cried out "Jesus! I'm coming to see you!" He knew he was going to die. As a soldier, he was trained to never quit, but he surrendered in that moment. He thought, Okay Lord, if this is how I am going to die, then okay. He shut his eyes and thought of his wife Mel, and their son Matt. He realized, he would never see them again.

In that moment, lying on the floor, engulfed in flames, he felt complete peace, no worries, no fear...just peace.

He knew he was going to die and soon would get to meet Jesus. In fact, he said that in those moments of being cooked alive, he felt God's presence stronger than at any other moment in his life. He was ready to go, and waited for death to come.

He waited.

And waited.

But he did not die. He lay there in terrible agony awaiting his death, but it would not come. God would not take his life even though he was ready.

After he waited, and prayed for a while, he began to feel something running down his face.

Blood?

Yes, there certainly was blood covering his face, but that wasn't what he felt.

What he felt was water.

He hadn't realized that the sprinkler system had gone off. He was so melted by fire, he could not feel the water hitting his back.

Only when it reached the portions of his face that were not terribly burned could he feel the water. Although he could only feel it run down his face, he knew it was hitting his entire body because the fire eventually ceased. His entire body was still steaming and burned, but there was no more fire. He couldn't feel relief because like the coals at the bottom of a camp fire... he was burning within, although there was no longer a fire on the outside. In his last attempt to reach safety, Col. Birdwell literally used every last ounce of strength he had to force himself to his knees, then to his feet, and began to walk.

He forced his mind to take control of his body and move forward. Every movement sent a jolt of unbearable pain through his body. Incredibly, he made his way to an exit door only to find it hidden behind fallen debris leaving access impossible. He tried to think of another way out, but this door was the only way. He was trapped again, and he felt it. He knew he was going to die, he had no more strength. He began to pray again. Still in agony he thought to himself 'am I ever going to die?'

More than ten minutes had passed since American Airlines Flight 77 exploded into the Pentagon; and it was the most agonizing time of Birdwell's life. Then, only by the grace of God and His almighty hand, Brian saw a door from the end of the corridor swing open and Colonel Roy Wallace stepped through to search the area. Brian immediately thought, Thank God! I'm saved!

Roy immediately noticed Brian and started toward him. Next coming through the door was Colonel Bill McKinnon, who knew Brian very well. They were students at the Command and General Staff College in Fort Leavenworth, and started at the Pentagon together. They would go on runs together and talk about their day. They spent a lot of time together and became like brothers.

But when Bill saw Brian, he did not recognize him. Brian was pitch black because of the burns and the soot and the debris and the ash and the blood that covered his body. Six people rushed over to pull him out of this living hell, but as they began to pick him up, his skin that had burned and become crusted began to slide and peel off of his body. Brian would later say he felt like a hotdog left on the grill too long, meaty on the inside but when you touch the outside it begins to flake off.

Birdwell began screaming for them not to touch him, but the six men clasped their hands underneath him, creating a stretcher with their arms as they picked him up and began to carry him out of the building. They had called for a medical personnel member to check the extent of Brian's injuries.

An IV was inserted through his foot, one of the only unburned areas on his body. Brian kept telling anyone who would listen to call his wife Mel and tell her he was alive. He ended up giving his wedding ring to Bill, who found who he was later.

The damage was so significant, Brian could not be physically identified by his features and all his ID cards had been melted into what little clothes he had left or what little skin he had left.

At this point, Brian began to feel even worse pain than when he was on fire because now he knew he wasn't going to die. He now found it impossible not to focus on the pain.

Working their way through corridors, hallways and courtyards, they finally got Brian out of the Pentagon and to more medical care. The more they moved him, the more they put him at risk of going into cardiac arrest. Brian looked down at his arm and saw flesh dangling from it and chunks of bloody skin falling off and he began to go into shock. The medical staff tried to calm him down and a women on her way out stopped and began to pray with Brian, and read Scripture.

Amidst the chaos, just enough medical staff was able to get their hands on Brian to keep him alive until they were able to borrow a car for a ride to the hospital. The ride to the hospital was only five minutes, but every bump, big or small, sent jolts of pain through Brian's entire body. After getting moved around from gurney to gurney, and room to room, he finally was placed in ICU in Georgetown hospital, where he would spend a very long time in rehabilitation and recovery.

———————————

As bad as 9/11 was, it was just the beginning of Birdwell's horrors. Every day, he endured scrubbings to get rid of the burnt skin and his entire body would be washed down. The recovery was often more painful than the flames.

He endured more than thirty surgeries, five on his face alone, and each one left scars he would live with forever. For the first several months he was on life support. He had a tube to help him breathe and eat, and fluids were constantly being put into his body to help him stay hydrated so his body would accept the new skin grafts. He became addicted to pain medication, but with the help of God and his wife, he was able to beat that and stay a faithful soldier.

The worst thing of all was wondering why God allowed him to suffer. Many times he asked God to let him die. But little did he know how God was going to use this horrific terrorist act and the outcome of his situation to touch thousands of others. God had a plan to use Brian's testimony to influence and encourage those who are going though difficulties. Hearing his story helps others to re-evaluate their own trials.

He applied Christ to everything he had experienced and began sharing Him with everyone he met. After learning that Cheryle and Sandi had not survived the attack, Brian realized he did not know where they stood with their salvation. He made a promise to Jesus that from the first day he left the hospital, he would spend time in every conversation speaking of the Lord and being a disciple for Him.

Spreading the Word of God became the number one priority for Brian, and his ministry grew out of that passion. Face the Fire Ministries has touched and healed tens of thousands of people across the nation. Lt. Col. Birdwell and his wife, Mel, have worked hard to live out the love of Christ and minister to those facing challenges that seem impossible to overcome. When Brian tells his story to those in difficult situations they are given new hope, and know that with God's help they too can have victory.

Brian and Mel speak all over America. He also serves as a Texas State Senator, after winning a very hard fought campaign. Just the fact that he is able to travel and do all that he does on a daily basis, is astounding.

Birdwell has had to overcome some very difficult challenges in the aftermath of 9/11. He has had to relearn many of the physical activities most of us take for granted, from being able to extend his arms fully, to just using the restroom on his own. After much perseverance and God's Grace, he is now capable of doing these things and much more.

In fact, he even works out on a regular basis!

It has not been an easy ride. Through every bump and crack in the road he and Mel pushed on until they reached their new destination, a life serving God. Through it all they have been there for each other and for their son Matt. Matt was only twelve-years-old when 9/11 happened, and had a hard time dealing with the trauma of hearing that his dad might die from his injuries. But like his parents, Matt pushed through the feelings and the challenges and life eventually became normal again.

As a family, they worked together with the support and love of Jesus Christ. They pulled through an immense tragedy and built it into a ministry, which is a positive force for good for so many people.

⚶ LIFE LESSONS

Whenever you think that the fire you're facing is going to engulf you and you can't escape, force yourself up, and get moving. Like Col. Birdwell, you may not be able to feel anything and it may seem hopeless, but remember, if you muster every last bit of strength you have, and don't give in, God will open doors for you, he will provide you a means of escape.

Even now, God is working in you for the better and He is probably doing it in ways you cannot currently recognize. A few weeks before 9/11, Brian bought a new pair of shoes, which he was wearing that day. Wearing those new shoes instead of his old worn out ones, helped save his life. The fire from the explosion left his feet untouched, and allowed him to receive the crucial IV. God provides a means of escape even when we are unaware of the method He is developing.

Shortly after the crash, someone shut down power to the corridor where Brian was literally burning alive. So, how were Roy Wallace and Bill McKinnon able to use their ID cards and gain access through the door they came through to get to Brian? It could only be opened with a card, which needed electricity to operate! How were they able to get that door open? Only one answer—God prepared a way.

God cares about us and pays attention even to the smallest detail. Col. Birdwell's situation is living proof that God is not only prepared to help in the time we need it most, but even well before our tough times. He is working a plan to make sure those future miracles are possible.

So when it feels like God is not paying attention, or He doesn't care, think about Brian in the moment when he was most ready to go, to die. God would not let him because that was not part of God's ultimate plan. He planned to use this horrible experience for good.

I believe that all things work together for good, and they do. God doesn't let evil happen just to happen, he lets it happen because something bigger and better is in His plan. Brian was a great man before 9/11, but he would not be able to touch and influence as many people today if it was not for the fact that he stood within twenty feet of the impact of corridor 4, and God wouldn't let him die.

God has a plan for all of us.

"Duty is ours; results are God's."
- John Adams.

LEGEND 10

DICEY LANGSTON

VOICED BY:

ALEXANDRA MURPHY

132

The legend of Dicey Langston is told by Alexandra Murphy.

Alexandra wrote her first published novel at only sixteen years old. Like the subject of her chapter here, Alexandra is fearless when it comes to standing for truth. She represents a new generation of patriots, outnumbered in a culture where truth and liberty are undervalued and cast aside. She, and the remnant of which she is a member, is the real hope for restoring the American values which have been too often trampled and abandoned by her parent's and grandparent's generations.

Like Legend #7 (Sybil Ludington voiced by Kamryn Green), Dicey's remarkable story is told in "faction" or "historical fiction" style in the way that Alexandra imagines it most likely occurred.

Dicey Langston is a legend of liberty who braved impossible odds and tremendous danger to help protect her fellow patriots. She was blessed to live a full life of liberty and raise a large family of patriots to which she passed the torch of freedom.

- Rick Green

Laodicea "Dicey" Langston
Born May 14, 1766.

Fifteen-year-old Laodicea Langston braved the rushing currents of the Tyger river with nothing but the moonlight to illuminate the path she'd made for herself. Known as 'Dicey' to all who beloved her, the loneliness of her daunting task settled in as she was reminded of the urgency with which she carried out this mission. "Don't stop, don't stop," she whispered between chilled breaths and strategically placed steps; if she stopped before the bank- the stream would surely sweep her away, and if she stopped anytime after reaching land she'd risk the Tories finding her- and that would be the more painful end of the two.

Trudging through two feet of water would normally be an easy endeavor, but this two-feet of water was moving so fast she could barely lift her leg up without being swept away. Toward the last stretch of the stream, Dicey lost her footing and plummeted into the murky depths. She emerged, but not without having lost her sense of direction first. Dicey gasped for air, the cloth of her dress having been caught on some drift, she succumbed to the water once more before finally pulling herself up onto the bank.

With her face in the sand, soaked to the bone, and aching all over, Dicey let herself rest only a few minutes. After allowing herself the short reprieve, Dicey picked herself up, wiped off what she could from her dirtied skirts, and steeled herself to finish her midnight run. Dicey's destination was the settlement of Little Eden, South Carolina, where her brother, James Langston, was camped; she intended to warn them about the attack that was set to happen around Daybreak by the 'Bloody Scouts.'

Dicey made it to James' door just in time. With great haste, she banged on the entrance and was quick to ignore his surprise at seeing her drenched from head to toe. James Langston settled his gun to his shoulder and listened as she delivered her message, his eyes wide by the end of it. They both began to spread the word to each ends of the camp, and men took up their arms in preparation for the threat.

Exhausted, Dicey eventually managed to take a step back from the chaos and breathe; she had done her job more than amiably, but her mission didn't stop here. Dicey had managed to get into the settlement and warn the men, but getting out safely would be equally as challenging...for dawn approached, which promised more blood shed than she cared to think about. Satisfied that she could attempt her run home, Dicey headed for a different route down the Tyger river, since she didn't desire to re-trace her steps, should the 'Bloody Scouts' be closing in.

The second time she plunged herself into the cold river

almost seemed worse than the first. Worn and still exhausted from her first trek, Dicey struggled as she slugged through the water; stamina was important to her survival, and she was losing too much of it. Hope renewed however, when she saw an encampment of friendlies on the other side. Though it looked to her like these men had given up hope, their heads and feet bandaged, helping them gave her a reason to reach the next bank.

Dicey arrived and immediately set those who would listen to gathering up some boards from the old rooftops, in order to make a decent fire. Not only would she benefit from the warmth, but some measly ingredients were also available to her, and she'd put her cooking to good use; most of these men looked like they could use something other than gruel. They'd need their strength, if they too, like her brother's settlement, hoped to fend off the scouts.

Thankfully in the short time she'd been there, Dicey had managed to lift their spirits, and fill their bellies. The men she'd helped began sharpening up and she knew they'd no longer go down without a fight. Unfortunately, she had to keep moving, home was miles away and the sun was rising fast. When she reached the familiar grounds of her father's house, Dicey dumped her wet clothes aside, got dressed, combed back her hair, and made her father breakfast in the knick of time. No one would have expected that she had just accomplished something extraordinary.

The 'Bloody Scouts' invaded just as she predicted, and because of her warnings the camps had been emptied and the men spared from an unsuspecting slaughter. This daring feat would be Dicey's first, but not the last brave stand she'd make. Solomon Langston, Dicey's father, was a Whig: (Whigs supported the revolution and separation from Great Britain, while the Tories supported the British in the war and did not believe America should break away from England.)

The leader of the 'Bloody Scouts' was none other than Bill Cunningham, and he was less than pleased that their morning attack on Little Eden had failed. Naturally, he'd searched for people to blame within the Whig party, and came to the conclusion that he'd thoroughly enjoy pinning Solomon Langston for the intel breach. Cunningham had been suspicious of Langston and his family for quite some time, they had to be spies, so this was a simple excuse to put an end to it.

The daughter, Laodicea, especially got on his nerves, as Dicey had made a habit of often visiting her brothers, who were also involved in the social reformation, and therefore seldom ventured home due to people like Cunningham lurking about.

He saw to it that Dicey and Solomon Langston were accused of being spies. Solomon was threatened further by being told his daughter's actions would also fall on his head, should she step out of line. To prevent that from happening, Solomon ordered that the visits to her brothers be stopped and that Dicey refrain from getting involved further.

She obeyed, only to ease her father's growing apprehensions... but the facade didn't last long. The Langstons were no strangers to having been accused of being spies, and after the loss at Little Eden, it became clear who were to be blamed. Solomon was to be executed, along with his relatives, and the Tories wasted no time in going to raid the Langston house.

Solomon was an older gentleman and too proud to beg for his life when the Tories arrived. Curtly, he responded to their accusations by saying he'd had nothing to do with the attack on Little Eden going amiss, nor was he responsible for the information that had been leaked. The leader of the men sent to strip the house of it's valuables, believed Langston to be senile, guilty, and beyond redemption. The gun was pointed at Solomon's chest before another thing could be said.

Dicey sprung to action. Being the more accurate target of their accusations, she threw herself between the two men and cradled her father to her bosom in a protective hold. Instead of confessing that she was the one that had warned the camp, Dicey had the gall to scold the man for pointing the pistol at her father! Enraged at being spoken to with such little respect, he warned her that the next shot would be placed at her own heart. Dicey continued to reprimanded the soldiers for their unruly behavior, claiming that her father was old and knew nothing of the incident. Her audacity and willingness to sacrifice herself for her father not only amused the Tories, but spared the Langstons. The gunman was called off and the remaining soldiers left, with no serious damage having been done to the family or the estate.

Being the passionate teenager she was, Dicey had no regard for her own safety during any of these encounters. Her brave acts of Patriotism, and constant harassment of the opposing side, earned her the pseudonym "Daring Dicey".

Another notable instance of her courage occurred a bit later in the war, and yet again it involved a gun being pointed at her chest. This seemed to be the most popular response when it came to confronting the Langston girl.

Dicey was returning from the Spartanburg District one afternoon when she was intercepted by a company of Loyalists who demanded intelligence from where she'd just left. Dicey refused, unflinching when the Captain of the band took his pistol and held it to her chest.

The Loyalists demanded again that she disclose all the information on her person, or "Die in her tracks." Unfazed by petty threats, Dicey replied with the calmness of a seasoned veteran. She puffed out her chest and whipped out a handkerchief, laying it across her clavicle, providing the Captain with a target in which to shoot. "Shoot me if you dare!" she said. "I will not tell you."

With clenched teeth, the Captain's finger rested against the trigger, barrel aimed at her chest. One press would silence her fiery tongue for good! Before he could fulfill that desire, another soldier's hand went up, and Dicey was spared.

Another occasion in which Darcy openly disregarded her safety happened a short time later when a rifle was left in her care by her brother James. She was instructed to keep the gun in her possession till her brother sent for it. James sent a group of "Liberty Men" to her father's house, in order to retrieve the rifle in his stead.

When they arrived, the broad-shouldered leader of the group

asked Dicey to retrieve the gun. Dicey went to retrieve it, but as she returned with the rifle, she realized she had not demanded the countersign that she and James had agreed upon. For all she knew, these men were Tories, and she could be in deep trouble.

Slowing her pace, Dicey clasped the gun to her chest and walked more quietly toward the group of men, who appeared just as wary of her as she was of them. The leader turned to her and she demanded the countersign, to which he didn't reply. "The gun is ours to posses, as we already posses the owner too!" He reached for the rifle, but Dicey jumped back and cocked it, aiming it toward his head.

Is that what you think?" Dicey closed one eye and lifted the rifle, presenting the muzzle to the leader. "If the gun is yours sir, take charge of her!" She gripped it tight, determined to shoot them if they tried to take it.

Seeing that she was earnest, the leader smirked and without further hesitation finally delivered the countersign. The men around him chuckled, and everyone agreed that she was indeed worthy of her reputation, and of her title as James' sister. The men collected the rifle from her and went to leave, but the leader of the "Liberty Men" stopped at the doorway, lingering for a bit longer than the rest of his group.

Thomas Springfield turned to Dicey and offered a smile. By facing them bravely in the face of uncertainty, she had earned his respect and admiration. Dicey offered him a sheepish grin in return for his attentions, there was a rare beauty to her smile. For a fearless girl who'd encountered and evaded death more than once— a wink and a wave of a hat from this man shouldn't have made her heart quicken like it did, but Thomas stirred something in her that would not be forgotten. Fast forward: January 6th, 1783— Dicey Langston married Thomas Springfield after the war.

For years after this memorable encounter with the "Liberty men," Dicey continued to live and breathe as a patriot. Unfortunately, the story of her courage and bravery is rarely taught in schools, but those who are fortunate enough to hear her story are refreshed by this young girl's zeal for her country.

A great verse to go along with Dicey Langston's story is 1 Timothy 4:12:

"Let no one despise you for your youth, but set the believers an example in speech, in conduct, in love, in faith, in purity." (English Standard Version)

Dicey is a perfect example of a young person who did not let anyone stop her because of her age. She was an example of patriotism, passion, and love for America and family. She had 23 children with her husband, Thomas Springfield, and was proud to have thrice as many grandchildren, who she happily claimed to all be readily armed Patriots. Dicey died on May 23rd on 1837 at the age of 71, having served her country till her last breath.

 **LIFE LESSONS:**

Dicey has inspired me personally to not let anything stop me because of my age. I am seventeen years old, and in comparison to Dicey, I have not yet done much for my country.

Like most young people in America today, I've held myself back too often, and I've second guessed myself far too much. But after researching Dicey, and taking note of her unfailing Patriotism and life of action, I feel rejuvenated and ready for a challenge. Like Dicey, I want to be an effective Patriot of America. I believe all of us, no matter our age, can learn the following lessons from the life of Dicey Langston:

1. Prepare ahead of time. Dicey was trained to handle firearms, she was well acquainted with the territory, and she paid attention to the political discussions around her so that she was informed. Had she waited to prepare until danger was literally at the door, she would have cowered to tyranny like most people. I want to better equip myself to serve this country. For me, that includes attending Patriot Academy and other opportunities to learn and equip myself to help restore the foundations of America, anywhere God can use me.

2. Strong families are absolutely essential to a strong nation. Dicey did not just rest on her own personal heroics. She raised up multiple generations of patriots ready to carry on the fight. Sometimes we can be so focused on our career or titles, that we forget the most important legacy we'll leave is through a strong family. When I'm older, I also hope to have many kids and grandkids who are armed patriots who will carry the torch in my stead, just like I know Dicey's children and grandchildren did.

2017 2nd Edition Editor's Note

Alexandra, our Legends biographer for Dicey, has a very similar story to Dicey. When she attended Patriot Academy for the first time, she faced off with a young man in fierce legislative debate over the issue of term limits. Two months after Legends of Liberty was first published in 2015, Alexandra married that fellow patriot - Trey Green, another Legends biographer. Just a few months after this 2nd Edition is to be published, they are expecting their first child, which will be my first grandchild!

- Rick Green

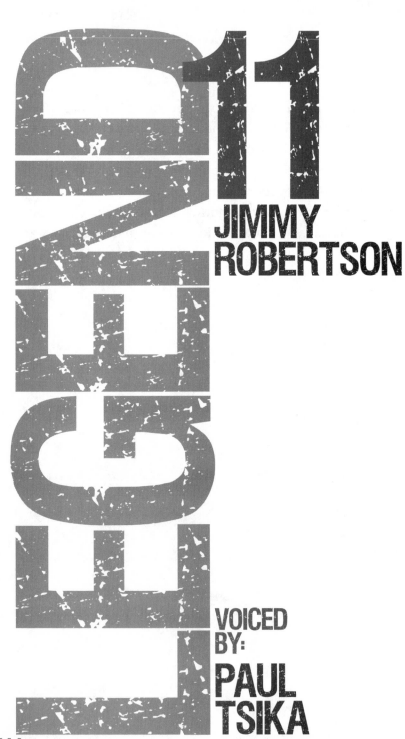

LEGEND 11

JIMMY
ROBERTSON

VOICED
BY:
PAUL
TSIKA

The legend of Jimmy Robertson is told by Pastor Paul Tsika.

Paul and Billie Kaye Tsika are two of the most amazing people on the planet and they have had a tremendous influence on our family. Paul serves on the board of Patriot Academy, so we have the opportunity to work closely in raising up a new generation of leaders. He and Billy Kaye continue to be mentors to Kara and me in every single area of our lives, from family and spiritual to business and finances, their wisdom and investment in our lives has been incalculable.

Paul and Billie Kaye's ministry, Restoration Ranch, and their books on marriage and parenting have saved thousands of marriages. Visit PlowOn.org to get their amazing, life building tools and learn more about this incredible family.

Jimmy Robertson is a Legend of Liberty for his role as an American pastor, mentor, and publisher, spreading the message of true liberty to multiple generations.

- Rick Green

"There Was A Man"

There are so many categories that could qualify as a 'hero category': Great statesmen, businessmen, inventors, explorers, builders, sports figures and on and on. There are men and women I admire from all of these categories that have great accomplishments. I've known businessmen that have become such a blessing to me that I'd have to put them in the category along with statesman and builders. However my "Legend of Liberty" is in a different category, altogether. He has been used by God as an instrument of liberty for tens of thousands of people throughout the world. The liberty I speak of is ultimately the only kind that matters: The liberty that Christ Jesus brings in salvation.

The word hero by definition means 'a man admired for his achievements and noble qualities'. or 'one who shows great courage'. At the age of 72 I must look back at my formative years as a preacher to see my hero. Some of the greatest men and women I have known in life are in a category that stands apart for me. Those heroic people would be in the category of The Christian Faith.

When I think of men and women that I have admired as a personal hero in that category there are several names that come to mind. However, one name towers above all others: My friend and former pastor from 1975 to 1987, Pastor Jimmy Robertson. He was born January 2, 1936 in the small Louisiana town of Tickfaw located in Tangipahoa Parish. He was one of 10 children born to Ray and Edna Robertson.

His father was a dairy farmer and his mother an old fashion, hard working woman raising a great family.

When Bro. Jimmy was 14 years old his father and brother took the family to a Revival meeting being held in a nearby town. It was there that Bro. Jimmy first heard the Gospel of Jesus Christ. That Christ died for him, and in his place and because of him. Convicted by the Holy Spirit, he found himself out back behind an old dairy barn crying out to God for mercy and grace. The following Sunday he found his way to church so that he could publicly profess faith in Christ. Over the next several years, his love for Christ and his passion for prayer and service grew as he attended Zion Hill Baptist church. By the time he was 18 years of age, he had surrendered to God's call on his life to the ministry. Preaching the Word of God became his greatest passion at a very young age. Old fashion tent meetings and street preaching were part of that passion. It was always more than just preaching with Jimmy, it was his faithfulness to the message of repentance and seeing the Holy Spirit of God transform lives. His preaching was the kind of message that attracted men, real men, with a love for Christ. All through the state of Louisiana God used him in a measure of true revival. The hand of God was upon his life and the breath of God was upon his preaching. He was as he is today, an uncompromising, fearless, faithful preacher of the good news of the Gospel. He certainly could echo the words of the Apostle Paul in I Corinthians 2:4, "And my speech and my preaching was not with enticing words of man's wisdom, but in demonstration of the Spirit and of power: That your faith should not stand in the wisdom of men, but in the power of God." He was not the most eloquent, the most educated or the most likely for God to use, but he is a man after God's own heart with a vision and burden for fresh moves of the Spirit. At 79 years of age he is still preaching, and that burden and vision have never faded from his life.

I'm sorry to say that I did not know Bro Jimmy in those early years. I first met him in 1974 in Chateau de Switzerland. He was part of a Bible conference being conducted there by several pastor friends. In our very first conversation, I knew this was a Man of God: A man of like passion as Elias was: A man of prayer and action: A man with a backbone like a saw log that would not back up, back down or back away from the truth. He was also a man of great compassion with a tender heart of forgiveness. He had a vision to reach the world with the gospel of Jesus Christ. As he shared his vision with me, it ignited a passion in my heart for the same.

Soon after our first meeting in Switzerland, he invited me to attend and speak at one of Milldale's Bible Camp meetings he had founded in 1964. These anointed camp meetings had been another vision birthed in the heart of Bro. Jimmy. The people of God came from every state to meet with the Lord. Several times a year people would gather on 17 acres outside Zachary, Louisiana, for no other purpose than to experience a move of God's Holy Spirit that would transform lives. Later that year, when my wife and I attended our first camp meeting, we knew we were home. That old tabernacle that was previously a bowling alley in downtown Baton Rouge was permeated with the presence of God. Engineers said it couldn't be moved and erected, but they had never met a man like Jimmy Robertson. He's always believed that NOTHING is impossible with God. The favor of God was obvious in those meetings and the atmosphere was charged with His glory. As I stood to speak on a Wednesday morning, I could hear in my mind the echoes of the great men and women who had ministered there. Most every noted speaker of the last two generations have either attended or spoken at Milldale's conferences. Even successful business men like Cecil Day, the founder of the Day's Inn Hotel chain, have shared their testimonies there and invested in Milldale's ministries. After the meeting Bro Jimmy extended a gracious invitation for our family to move to Milldale and work out from their church as an Evangelist. As a young Evangelist with only 5 meetings scheduled my faith was elevated by this unusual man. Jimmy had laid a fleece before God and within 2 days God answered, giving me more assurance. I moved my family to Milldale that fall, and we were blessed for 15 years of fruitful ministry and friendships. Bro Jimmy was a father to our children as I traveled, and he watched over my family as his own.

As my pastor, he demonstrated to me, daily, what it meant to labor in God's vineyard. Along with his godly wife Frances they not only blessed and cared for our family, they labored and ministered side by side until he passed on the mantel of leadership in 2004.

Bro Jimmy founded Milldale Baptist Church, Milldale Bible

Conference, Fires of Revival paper and Milldale International Ministries. This ministry alone has been responsible for distributing over ONE BILLION, with a "B", pieces of Christian literature around the world. Until the iron curtain came down, Milldale International Ministries printed more Bible literature for Communist countries than any other Christian organization in America. Bibles, tracts, books and other literature were sent free of charge for multiplied years to those countries.

Milldale Baptist Church has been the foundation for many outreaches, including Milldale Bible Conference and Fires of Revival paper, to bless the Christian community. Several times a year, this paper was mailed free to every Baptist church in America. Articles of encouragement and edification were written to challenge Christians to genuine revival. Thousand's have been saved, made right with God, surrendered to preach and sent to the mission field under the ministry of Milldale's Bible conferences. Tens of thousands have been fed and housed free on the grounds for over 50 years, and all because a young man from Tickfaw, Louisiana, was visited by the Holy Ghost behind an old dairy barn.

Often times Bro Jimmy would find himself shut up to God for a time of prayer and fasting.. in a hunting camp for days... near the swamps...with only a jug of water. He would emerge with a word from God and direction for the church, missions and the camp meetings.

When Bro. Jimmy preached on missions you wanted to sell every thing you had and lay it on the altar. Time and time again we would end up shaking our heads over God's provision.

Monies would come from totally unexpected sources for paper to print Bibles or make needed repairs on the grounds. We witnessed God's power and longed for more. There is not enough space to testify of the countless interventions when God visited us. Miracles were frequent and unexplainable.

Revival and the breath of God would come upon that old tabernacle over and over again. Genuine miracles, manifestations of God's presence and an atmosphere that mortal tongue can not describe were the norm. Grounds filled with Believers praying, crying out and seeking the face of God could be heard from down the street. The little prayer Chapel was filled day and night with intercessory prayer while meetings were being conducted. You just had to be there and even then words would fail you.

Time and space would fail to describe how God raised up and used this man. Although his life has been somewhat hid in obscurity, I know the Lord has recorded a faithful ministry. I also know, because of his humility, that's the way he prefers. He will probably never receive the recognition he so rightfully deserves on this side of eternity, but he's never sought that recognition or attention from the Christian community. The only acknowledgement he's concerned himself with is the amen and favor of a Holy God upon his life and work.

What have I learned from my friend and mentor: Lessons that have followed me to this day.

No matter who you are or where you come from, God can greatly use you.

The anointing of God must be sought over the applause of men.

Genuine Revival comes from God alone and cannot be manipulated by man.

Education, while important, can never replace the knowledge of God's Word and knowing God in the power of His resurrection and the fellowship of His suffering.

The work of God will survive and thrive with or without you, but God allows you the blessing of partnership with Him.

Most frustrations in ministry come from your unwillingness to allow God to set the lever of your ministry.

What books and people have to say about the Word of God is never as powerful as the Word of God itself, so preach the Word.

Don't ever judge men, because you never know when you're not around them if they have repented and been made right with God.

Trusting God is not optional.

You may win the argument but winning the man is more important.

The Word of God needs the breath of God to bring it to life.

Missions is the very heart of God

Your mission and dream need to be big enough that nothing short of a miracle of God will suffice.

With greater leadership comes greater responsibility.

God's work done in God's way never lacks for God's support.

NOTHING IS IMPOSSIBLE WITH GOD

Oh, and one more thing. We were riding together one day driving from Baton Rouge to Houston. I was talking seemingly without taking a breath. Finally he turned to me and said, "You don't have to talk all the time..." One of the hardest lessons I've tried to learn. Although a serious man he loves to laugh, and he has a great sense of humor.

There is so much more I have learned that could be said of this man of God. I feel like the Queen of Sheba when she saw the wealth of Solomon and said, "the half has never been told."

And so, I'm thankful to have this opportunity to honor a man that I have always loved deeply, and count as my greatest influence for Christ and my father in the faith. For 15 years we lived and labored side by side and were inseparable. He taught and demonstrated more to me about Christianity in those years than I have learned before or since. Even thought we moved from Louisiana in 1987, no amount of time or distance can ever depreciate my love, respect and appreciation for this man of God. After 28 years I'm thrilled to acknowledge him for the contribution he's made to my life, family and ministry. My dear friend, pastor, mentor and hero, Jimmy Robertson, thank you for being there for me.

LEGEND

12

JOHN LOCKE

VOICED
BY:

**DAVID
BARTON**

The legend of John Locke is told by David Barton.

(see Chapter 2 for my initial introduction of David)

As a student of the American founding and perhaps having read more of the writings of the founding fathers than any other living person, David has a very good grasp of what most influenced the founders of America.

John Locke is a Legend of Liberty whose significant influence on the founding of America is a very large part of why we enjoy liberty today.

- Rick Green

John Locke
(1632-1704)

John Locke is one of the most important, but largely unknown names in American history today. A celebrated English philosopher, educator, government official, and theologian, it is not an exaggeration to say that without his substantial influence on American thinking, there might well be no United States of America today – or at the very least, America certainly would not exist with the same level of rights, stability of government, and quality of life that we have enjoyed for well over two centuries.

Historians – especially of previous generations – were understandably effusive in their praise of Locke. For example:

- In 1833, Justice Joseph Story, author of the famed *Commentaries on the Constitution*, described Locke as "a most strenuous asserter of liberty"[1] who helped establish in this country the sovereignty of the people over the government,[2] majority rule with minority protection,[3] and the rights of conscience.[4]

• In 1834, George Bancroft, called the "Father of American History," described Locke as "the rival of 'the ancient philosophers' to whom the world had 'erected statues',"[5] and noted that Locke esteemed "the pursuit of truth the first object of life and... never sacrificed a conviction to an interest."[6]

• In 1872, historian Richard Frothingham said that Locke's principles – principles that he said were "inspired and imbued with the Christian idea of man" – produced the "leading principle [of] republicanism" that was "summed up in the Declaration of Independence and became the American theory of government."[7]

• In the 1890s, John Fiske, the celebrated nineteenth-century historian, affirmed that Locke brought to America "the idea of complete liberty of conscience in matters of religion" allowing persons with "any sort of notion about God" to be protected "against all interference or molestation,"[8] and that Locke should "be ranked in the same order with Aristotle."[9]

Such acknowledgments continued across the generations; and even over the past half century, U. S. presidents have also regularly acknowledged America's debt to John Locke:

• President Richard Nixon affirmed that "John Locke's concept of 'life, liberty and property'" was the basis of "the inalienable rights of man" in the Declaration of Independence.[10]

• President Gerald Ford avowed that "Our revolutionary

leaders heeded John Locke's teaching 'Where there is no law, there is no freedom'."[11]

• President Ronald Reagan confirmed that much in America "testif[ies] to the power and the vision of free men inspired by the ideals and dedication to liberty of John Locke..."[12]

• President Bill Clinton reminded the British Prime Minister that "Throughout our history, our peoples have reinforced each other in the living classroom of democracy. It is difficult to imagine Jefferson, for example, without John Locke before him."[13]

• President George W. Bush confessed that "We're sometimes faulted for a naive faith that liberty can change the world, [but i]f that's an error, it began with reading too much John Locke..."[14]

The influence of Locke on America was truly profound; he was what we now consider to be a renaissance man – an individual skilled in numerous areas and diverse subjects. He had been well-educated and received multiple degrees from some of the best institutions of his day, but he also pursued extensive self-education in the fields of religion, philosophy, education, law, and government – subjects on which he authored numerous substantial works, most of which still remain in print today more than three centuries after he published them.

In 1689, Locke penned his famous *Two Treatises of Government*. The first treatise (i.e., a thorough examination) was a brilliant Biblical refutation of Sir Robert Filmer's *Patriarcha* in which Filmer had attempted to produce Biblical support for the errant "Divine Right of Kings" doctrine. Locke's second treatise set forth the fundamental principles defining the proper role, function, and operation of a sound government. Significantly, Locke had ample opportunity to assert such principles, for he spent time under some of England's worst monarchs, including Charles I, Charles II, and James II.

In 1664, Locke penned "Questions Concerning the Law of Nature" in which he asserted that human reason and Divine revelation were fully compatible and were not enemies – that the Law of Nature actually came from God Himself. (This work was not published, but many of its concepts appeared in his subsequent writings.)

In 1667, he privately penned his "Essay Concerning Toleration," first published in 1689 as *A Letter Concerning Toleration*. This work, like his *Two Treatises*, was published anonymously, for it had placed his very life in danger by directly criticizing and challenging the frequent brutal oppression of the government-established and government-run Church of England. (Under English law, the Anglican Church and its 39 Doctrinal Articles were the measure for all religious faith in England; every citizen was required to attend an Anglican Church. Dissenters who opposed those Anglican requirements were regularly persecuted or even killed. Locke objected to the government establishing specific church doctrines by law, argued for a separation of the state from the church, and urged religious toleration for those who did not adhere to Anglican doctrines.) When Locke's position on religious toleration was attacked by defenders of the government-run church, he responded with *A Second Letter Concerning Toleration* (1690), and then *A Third Letter for Toleration* (1692) – both also published anonymously.

In 1690, Locke published his famous *Essay Concerning Human Understanding*. This work resulted in him being called the "Father of Empiricism," which is the doctrine that knowledge is derived primarily from experience. Rationalism, on the other hand, places reason above experience; and while Locke definitely did not oppose reason, his approach to learning was more focused on the practical, whereas rationalism was more focused on the theoretical.

In 1693, Locke published *Some Thoughts Concerning Education*. Originally a series of letters written to his friend concerning the education of a son, in them Locke suggested the best ways to educate children. He proposed a three-pronged holistic approach to education that included (1) a regimen of bodily exercise and maintenance of physical health (that there should be "a sound mind in a sound body"[15]), (2) the development of a virtuous character (which he considered to be the most important element of education), and (3) the training of the mind through practical and useful academic curriculum (also encouraging students to learn a practical trade). Locke believed that education made the individual – that "of all the men we meet with, nine parts of ten are what they are, good or evil, useful or not, by their education."[16] This book became a run-away best-seller, being printed in nearly every European language and going through 53 editions over the next century.

Locke's latter writings focused primarily on theological subjects, including *The Reasonableness of Christianity as Delivered in the Scriptures* (1695), *A Vindication of the*

Reasonableness of Christianity (1695), *A Second Vindication of the Reasonableness of Christianity* (1697), *A Common-Place-Book to the Holy Bible* (1697), which was a re-publication of what he called *Graphautarkeia, or, The Scriptures Sufficiency Practically Demonstrated* (1676), and finally *A Paraphrase and Notes on the Epistles of St. Paul to the Galatians, 1 and 2 Corinthians, Romans, Ephesians* (published posthumously in 1707).

In his *Reasonableness of Christianity*, Locke urged the Church of England to reform itself so as to allow inclusion of members from other Christian denominations – i.e., the Dissenters. He recommended that the Church place its emphasis on the major things of Christianity (such as an individual's relationship with Jesus Christ) rather than on lesser things (such as liturgy, church hierarchy and structure, and form of discipline). That work also defended Christianity against the attacks of skeptics and secularists, who had argued that Divine revelation must be rejected because truth could be established only through reason.

(While these are some of Locke's better known works, he also wrote on many other subjects, including poetry and literature, medicine, commerce and economics, and even agriculture.)

The impact of Locke's writings had a direct and substantial influence on American thinking and behavior in both the religious and the civil realms – an influence especially visible in the years leading up to America's separation from Great Britain. In fact, the Founding Fathers openly acknowledged their debt to Locke:

- John Adams praised Locke's *Essay on Human Understanding*, openly acknowledging that "Mr. Locke... has steered his course into the unenlightened regions of the human mind, and like Columbus, has discovered a new world."[17]

- Declaration signer Benjamin Rush said that Locke was not only "an oracle as to the principles... of government"[18] (an "oracle" is a wise authority whose opinions are not questioned) but that in philosophy, he was also a "justly celebrated oracle, who first unfolded to us a map of the intellectual world,"[19] having "cleared this sublime science of its technical rubbish and rendered it both intelligible and useful."[20]

- Benjamin Franklin said that Locke was one of "the best English authors" for the study of "history, rhetoric, logic, moral and natural philosophy."[21]

- Noah Webster, a Founding Father called the "Schoolmaster to America," directly acknowledged Locke's influence in establishing sound principles of education.[22]

- James Wilson (a signer of the Declaration and the Constitution, and an original Justice on the U. S. Supreme Court) declared that "The doctrine of toleration in matters of religion . . . has not been long known or acknowledged. For its reception and establishment (where it has been received and established), the world has been thought to owe much to the inestimable writings of the celebrated Locke..."[23]

- James Monroe, a Founding Father who became the fifth President of the United States, attributed much of our constitutional philosophy to Locke, including our belief that "the division of the powers of a government . . . into three branches (the legislative, executive, and judiciary) is absolutely necessary for the preservation of liberty."[24]

• Thomas Jefferson said that Locke was among "my trinity of the three greatest men the world had ever produced."[25]

And just as the Founding Fathers regularly praised and invoked John Locke, so, too, did numerous famous American ministers in their writings and sermons.[26] Locke's influence was substantial; and significantly, the closer came the American Revolution, the more frequently he was invoked.

For example, in 1775, Alexander Hamilton recommended that anyone wanting to understand the thinking in favor of American independence should "apply yourself without delay to the study of the law of nature. I would recommend to your perusal... Locke."[27]

And James Otis – the mentor of both Samuel Adams and John Hancock – affirmed that:

The authority of Mr. Locke has... been preferred to all others.[28]

Locke's specific writing that most influenced the American philosophy of government was his *Two Treatises of Government*. In fact, signer of the Declaration Richard Henry Lee saw the Declaration of Independence as being "copied from Locke's *Treatise on Government*"[29] – and modern researchers agree, having authoritatively documented that not only was John Locke one of three most-cited political philosophers during the Founding Era[30] but that he was by far the single most frequently-cited source in the years from 1760-1776 (the period leading up to the Declaration of Independence).[31]

Among the many ideas articulated by Locke that subsequently appeared in the Declaration was the theory of social compact, which, according to Locke, was when:

> Men... join and unite into a community for their comfortable, safe, and peaceable living one amongst another in a secure enjoyment of their properties and a greater security against any that are not of it.[32]

Of that theory, William Findley, a Revolutionary soldier and a U. S. Congressman, explained:

> Men must first associate together before they can form rules for their civil government. When those rules are formed and put in operation, they have become a civil society, or organized government. For this purpose, some rights of individuals must have been given up to the society but repaid many fold by the protection of life, liberty, and property afforded by the strong arm of civil government. This progress to human happiness being agreeable to the will of God, Who loves and commands order, is the ordinance of God mentioned by the Apostle Paul and . . . the Apostle Peter.[33]

Locke's theory of social compact is seen in the Declaration's phrase that governments "derive their just powers from the consent of the governed."

Locke also taught that government must be built firmly upon the transcendent, unchanging principles of natural law that were merely a subset of God's greater law:

> [T]he Law of Nature stands as an eternal rule to all men, legislators as well as others. The rules that they make for other men's actions must... be conformable to the Law of Nature, *i.e.*, to the will of God.[34]

> [L]aws human must be made according to the general laws of Nature, and without contradiction to any positive law of Scripture, otherwise they are ill made.[35]

> For obedience is due in the first place to God, and afterwards to the laws.[36]

The Declaration therefore acknowledges "the laws of nature <u>and</u> of nature's God," thus not separating the two but rather affirming their interdependent relationship – the dual connection between reason and revelation which Locke so often asserted.

Locke also proclaimed that certain fundamental rights should be protected by society and government, including especially those of life, liberty, and property[37] – three rights specifically listed as God-given inalienable rights in the Declaration. As Samuel Adams (the "Father of the American Revolution" and a signer of the Declaration) affirmed, man's inalienable rights included "first, a right to life; secondly, to liberty; thirdly, to property"[38] – a repeat of Locke's list.

Locke had also asserted that:

> [T]he first and fundamental positive law of all
> commonwealths is the establishing of the Legislative
> power... [and no] edict of anybody else... [can] have the force
> and obligation of a law which has not its sanction [approval]
> from that Legislative which the public has chosen.[39]

The Founders thus placed a heavy emphasis on preserving legislative powers above all others. In fact, of the 27 grievances set forth in the Declaration of Independence, 11 dealt with the abuse of legislative powers – no other topic in the Declaration received nearly as much attention. The Founders' conviction that the Legislative Branch was above both the Executive and Judicial branches was also readily evident in the U. S. Constitution, with the *Federalist Papers* affirming that "the legislative authority necessarily predominates"[40] and "the judiciary is beyond comparison the weakest of the three departments of power."[41]

Locke also advocated the removal of a leader who failed to fulfill the basic functions of government so eloquently set forth in his *Two Treatises*;[42] the Declaration thus declares that "whenever any form of government becomes destructive of these ends, it is the right of the people to alter or to abolish it and to institute new government."

In short, when one studies Locke's writings and then reads the Declaration of Independence, they will agree with John Quincy Adams' pronouncement that:

> The Declaration of Independence [was]... founded upon
> one and the same theory of government... expounded in the
> writings of Locke.[43]

But despite Locke's substantial influence on America, today he is largely unknown; and his *Two Treatises* are no longer intimately studied in America history and government classes. Perhaps the reason for the modern dismissal of this classic work is because it was so thoroughly religious: Locke invoked the Bible in at least 1,349 references in the first treatise, and 157 times in the second[44] – a fact not lost on the Founders. As John Adams openly acknowledged:

> The general principles on which the Fathers achieved independence... were the general principles of Christianity... Now I will avow that I then believed (and now believe) that those general principles of Christianity are as eternal and immutable as the existence and attributes of God... In favor of these general principles in philosophy, religion, and government, I [c]ould fill sheets of quotations from... [philosophers including] Locke – not to mention thousands of divines and philosophers of inferior fame.[45]

Given the fact that previous generations so quickly recognized the Christian principles that permeated all of Locke's diverse writings, it is not surprising that they considered him a theologian.[46] Ironically, however, many of today's writers and so-called professors and scholars specifically call Locke a deist or a forerunner of Deism.[47] But since Locke included repeated references to God and the Scriptures throughout his writings, and since he wrote many works specifically in defense of religious topics, then why is he currently portrayed as being anti-religious? It is because in the past fifty-years, American education has become thoroughly infused with the dual historical malpractices of Deconstructionism and Academic Collectivism.

Deconstructionism is a philosophy that "tends to deemphasize or even efface [i.e., malign and smear] the subject" by posing "a continuous critique" to "lay low what was once high"[48] and "tear down the ancient certainties upon which Western Culture is founded."[49] In other words, it is a steady flow of belittling and negative portrayals about the heroes, institutions, and values of Western civilization, especially if they reflect religious beliefs. The two regular means by which Deconstructionists accomplish this goal are (1) to make a negative exception appear to be the rule, and (2) deliberate omission.

These harmful practices of Deconstructionists are exacerbated by the malpractice of Academic Collectivism, whereby scholars quote each other and those from their group rather than original sources. Too many writers today simply repeat what other modern writers say, and this "peer-review" becomes the standard for historical truth rather than an examination of actual original documents and sources.

Reflecting these dual negative influences of Deconstructionism and Academic Collectivism in their treatment of John Locke, many of today's "scholars" simply lift a few short excerpts from his hundreds of thousands of written words and then present those carefully selected extracts in such a way as to misconstrue his faith and make it seem that he was irreligious. Or more frequently, Locke's works are simply omitted from academic studies, being replaced only with a professor's often inaccurate characterization of Locke's beliefs and writings.

Significantly, the charge that Locke is a deist and a freethinker is not new; it has been raised against him for over three centuries. It first originated when Locke advocated major reforms in the

Church of England (such as the separation of the state from the church and the extension of religious toleration to other Christian denominations); Anglican apologists who stung from his biting criticism sought to malign him and minimize his influence; they thus accused him of irreligion and deism. As affirmed by early English theologian Richard Price:

> [W]hen... Mr. Locke's *Essay on the Human Understanding* was first published in Britain, the persons readiest to attend to it and to receive it were those who have never been trained in colleges, and whose minds, therefore, had never been perverted by an instruction in the jargon of the schools. [But t]o the deep professors [i.e., clergy and scholars] of the times, it appeared (like the doctrine taught in his book, on the *Reasonableness of Christianity*) to be a dangerous novelty and heresy; and the University of Oxford in particular [which trained only Anglicans] condemned and reprobated the author.[50]

The Founding Fathers were fully aware of the bigoted motives behind the attacks on Locke's Christian beliefs, and they vigorously defended him from those false charges. For example, James Wilson (signer of the Declaration and Constitution) asserted:

> I am equally far from believing that Mr. Locke was a friend to infidelity [a disbelief in the Bible and in Christianity[51]]... The high reputation which he deservedly acquired for his enlightened attachment to the mild and tolerating doctrines of Christianity secured to him the esteem and confidence of those who were its friends. The same high and deserved reputation inspired others of very different views and characters... to diffuse a fascinating kind of lustre over their own tenets of a

dark and sable hue. The consequence has been that the writings of Mr. Locke, one of the most able, most sincere, and most amiable assertors of Christianity and true philosophy, have been perverted to purposes which he would have deprecated and prevented [disapproved and opposed] had he discovered or foreseen them.[52]

Thomas Jefferson agreed. He had personally studied not only Locke's governmental and legal writings but also his theological ones; and his summary of Locke's views of Christianity clearly affirmed that Locke was not a deist. According to Jefferson:

Locke's system of Christianity is this: Adam was created happy and immortal... By sin he lost this so that he became subject to total death (like that of brutes [animals]) – to the crosses and unhappiness of this life. At the intercession, however, of the Son of God, this sentence was in part remitted... And moreover to them who *believed*, their *faith* was to be counted for righteousness [Romans 4:3,5]. Not that faith without works was to save them; St. James, chapter 2 says expressly the contrary [James 2:14-26]... So that a reformation of life (included under *repentance*) was essential, and defects in this would be made up by their *faith*; i. e., their faith should be counted for righteousness [Romans 4:3,5]... The Gentiles; St. Paul says, Romans 2:13: "the Gentiles have the law written in their hearts," [A]dding a *faith* in God and His attributes that on their repentance, He would pardon them; (1 John 1:9) they also would be justified (Romans 3:24). This then explains the text "there is no other *name* under heaven by which a man may be saved" [Acts 4:12], i. e., the defects in good works shall not be supplied by a faith in Mahomet, Fo [Buddha], or any other except Christ.[53]

In short, Locke was not the deist thinker that today's shallow and often lazy academics so frequently claim him to be; and although Locke is largely ignored today, his influence both on American religious and political thinking was substantial, directly shaping key beliefs upon which America was established and under which she continues to operate and prosper.

---

[1] Joseph Story, *Commentaries on the Constitution of the United States* (Boston: Hilliard, Gray, and Company 1833), Vol. I, p. 299, n2.

[2] Joseph Story, *Commentaries on the Constitution of the United States* (Boston: Hilliard, Gray, and Company 1833), Vol. II, p. 57, n2.

[3] Joseph Story, *Commentaries on the Constitution of the United States* (Boston: Hilliard, Gray, and Company 1833), Vol. I, p. 293, n2; p. 299, n2; pp. 305-306.

[4] Joseph Story, *Commentaries on the Constitution of the United States* (Boston: Hilliard, Gray, and Company 1833), Vol. III, p. 727.

[5] George Bancroft, *History of the United States of America* (Boston: Little, Brown, and Company, 1858; first edition Boston: Charles Bowen, 1834), Vol. II, p. 150.

[6] George Bancroft, *History of the United States of America* (Boston: Little, Brown, and Company, 1858; first edition Boston: Charles Bowen, 1834), Vol. II, p. 144.

[7] Richard Frothingham, *The Rise of the Republic of the United States* (Boston: Little, Brown, and Company, 1872), p. 165.

[8] John Fiske, *Old Virginia and Her Neighbors* (New York: Houghton, Mifflin and Company, 1897), Vol. II, p. 274.

[9] John Fiske, *Critical Period of American History*: 1783-1789 (New York: Mifflin and Company, 1896), p. 225.

[10] Richard Nixon, "Message to the Congress Transmitting the Report of the American Revolution Bicentennial Commission," *The American Presidency Project*, September 11, 1970 (at: http://www.presidency.ucsb.

edu/ws/index.php?pid=2658&st=John+Locke&st1=#ixzz1Vm7XvNfc).

[11] Gerald Ford, "Address at the Yale University Law School Sesquicentennial Convocation Dinner," *The American Presidency Project*, April 25, 1975 (at: http://www.presidency.ucsb.edu/ws/index.php?pid=4869&st=John+Locke&st1=#ixzz1Vm8RSZb1).

[12] Ronald Reagan, "Toasts of the President and Queen Elizabeth II of the United Kingdom at a Dinner Honoring the Queen in San Francisco, California," *The American Presidency Project*, March 3, 1983 (at: http://www.presidency.ucsb.edu/ws/index.php?pid=40996&st=John+Locke&st1=#ixzz1VmAxJTEw).

[13] William Clinton, "Remarks at the State Dinner Honoring Prime Minister Tony Blair of the United Kingdom," *The American Presidency Project*, February 5, 1998 (at: http://www.presidency.ucsb.edu/ws/index.php?pid=55226&st=John+Locke&st1=#ixzz1VmCqe1mq).

[14] George W. Bush, "Remarks at Whitehall Palace in London, United Kingdom," *The American Presidency Project*, November 19, 2003 (at: http://www.presidency.ucsb.edu/ws/index.php?pid=812&st=John+Locke&st1=#ixzz1VmDpUlFV).

[15] John Locke, *The Works of John Locke* (London: Arthur Bettesworth, John Pemberton, and Edward Simon, 1722), Vol. III, p. 1, "Some Thoughts Concerning Education."

[16] John Locke, *The Works of John Locke* (London: Arthur Bettesworth, John Pemberton, and Edward Simon, 1722), Vol. III, p. 1, "Some Thoughts Concerning Education."

[17] John Adams, *The Works of John Adams*, Charles Francis Adams, editor (Boston: Little, Brown and Company, 1856), Vol. I, p. 53, to Jonathan Sewall on February 1760.

[18] Benjamin Rush, *The Selected Writings of Benjamin Rush*, Dagobert D. Runes, editor (New York: The Philosophical Library, Inc., 1947), p. 78, "Observations on the Government of Pennsylvania."

[19] Benjamin Rush, *Medical Inquiries and Observations* (Philadelphia: T. Dobson, 1793), Vol. II, p. 17, "An Inquiry into the Influence of Physical Causes upon the Moral Faculty."

[20] Benjamin Rush, *Medical Inquiries and Observations* (Philadelphia: Thomas Dobson, 1794), Vol. I, p. 332, "Duties of a Physician."

[21] Benjamin Franklin, *The Works of Benjamin Franklin*, Jared Sparks, editor (Boston: Tappan & Whittemore, 1836), Vol. II, p. 131, "Sketch of

an English School."

²² Noah Webster, *A Collection of Papers on Political, Literary and Moral Subjects* (New York: Webster & Clark, 1843), p. 308, "Modes of Teaching the English Language."

²³ James Wilson, *The Works of the Honourable James Wilson*, Bird Wilson, editor (Philadelphia: Lorenzo Press, 1804), Vol. 1, pp. 6-7, "Of the Study of the Law in the United States."

²⁴ James Monroe, *The Writings of James Monroe*, Stanislaus Murray Hamilton, editor (New York: G. P. Putnam's Sons, 1898), Vol. I, p. 325, "Some Observations on the Constitution, &c."

²⁵ Thomas Jefferson, *The Writings of Thomas Jefferson*, Henry Augustine Washington, editor (Washington, D. C.: Taylor & Maury, 1853), Vol. V, p. 559, to Dr. Benjamin Rush on January 16, 1811.

²⁶ See, for example, REV. JARED ELIOT IN 1738 Jared Eliot, *Give Caesar His Due. Or, Obligation that Subjects are Under to Their Civil Rulers* (London: T. Green, 1738), p. 27, Evans # 4241. REV. ELISHA WILLIAMS IN 1744 Elisha Williams, *The Essential Rights and Liberties of Protestants. A Seasonable Plea for the Liberty of Conscience, and the Right of Private Judgment, in Matters of Religion* (Boston: S. Kneeland and T. Gaben, 1744), p. 4, Evans # 5520. REV. JONATHAN EDWARDS IN 1754 Jonathan Edwards, *A Careful and Strict Inquiry into the Modern Prevailing Notions of That Freedom of Will, which is Supposed to be Essential to Moral Agency, Virtue and Vice, Reward and Punishment, Praise and Blame* (Boston: S. Kneeland, 1754), pp. 138-140, 143, 164, 171-172, 353-354 (available online at: http://edwards.yale.edu/archive?path=aHR0cDovL2Vkd2FyZHMueWFsZS5lZHUvY2dpLWJpbi9uZXdwaGlsby9YZpZ2F0ZS5wbD93amVvLjA=). REV. WILLIAM PATTEN, 1766 William Patten, *A Discourse Delivered at Hallifax in the County of Plymouth, July 24th, 1766* (Boston: D. Kneeland, 1766), pp. 17-18n, Evans # 10440. REV. STEPHEN JOHNSON, 1766 Stephen Johnson, *Some Important Observations, Occasioned by, and Adapted to, the Publick Fast, Ordered by Authority, December 18th, A. D. 1765. On Account of the Peculiar Circumstances of the Present Day* (Newport: Samuel Hall, 1766), pp. 22n-23n, Evans # 10364. REV. JOHN TUCKER, 1771 John Tucker, *A Sermon Preached at Cambridge Before His Excellency Thomas Hutchinson, Esq., Governor; His Honor Andrew Oliver, Esq., Lieutenant-Governor; the Honorable His Majesty's Council; and the Honorable House of Representatives of the Province of the Massachusetts-Bay in New England, May 29th, 1771* (Boston: Richard

Draper, 1771), p. 19, Evans # 12256. Rev. Samuel Stillman, 1779 Samuel Stillman, *A Sermon Preached before the Honourable Council and the Honourable House of Representatives of the State of Massachusetts-Bay, in New-England at Boston, May 26, 1779. Being the Anniversary for the Election of the Honorable Council* (Boston: T. and J. Fleet, 1779), pp. 22-25, and many others.

[27] Alexander Hamilton, *The Papers of Alexander Hamilton*, Harold C. Syrett, editor (New York: Columbia University Press, 1961), Vol. I, p. 86, from "The Farmer Refuted," February 23, 1775.

[28] James Otis, *A Vindication of the Conduct of the House of Representatives of the Province on the Massachusetts-Bay: Most Particularly in the Last Session of the General Assembly* (Boston: Edes & Gill, 1762), p. 20n.

[29] Thomas Jefferson, *The Writings of Thomas Jefferson*, Andrew A. Lipscomb, editor (Washington, D.C.: The Thomas Jefferson Memorial Association, 1904), Vol. XV, p. 462, to James Madison on August 30, 1823.

[30] Donald S. Lutz, *The Origins of American Constitutionalism* (Baton Rouge: Louisiana State University Press, 1988), p. 143.

[31] Donald S. Lutz, *The Origins of American Constitutionalism* (Baton Rouge: Louisiana State University Press, 1988), p. 143.

[32] John Locke, *Two Treatises of Government* (London: A. Bettesworth, 1728), Book II, pp. 206-207, Ch. VIII, §95.

[33] William Findley, *Observations on "The Two Sons of Oil"* (Pittsburgh: Patterson and Hopkins 1812), p. 35.

[34] John Locke, *Two Treatises of Government* (London: A. Bettesworth, 1728), Book II, p. 233, Ch. XI, §135.

[35] John Locke, *Two Treatises of Government* (London: A. Bettesworth, 1728), Book II, p. 234, Ch. XI, §135 n., quoting Hooker's *Eccl. Pol.* 1. iii, sect. 9.

[36] John Locke, *The Works of John Locke* (London: T. Davison, 1824), Vol. V, "A Letter Concerning Toleration," p. 22.

[37] See, for example, John Locke, *The Works of John Locke* (London: T. Davison, 1824), Vol. V, p. 10, "A Letter Concerning Toleration"; John Locke, *Two Treatises of Government* (London: A. Bettesworth, 1728), Book II, pp. 146, 188, 199, 232-233, *passim*; etc.

[38] Samuel Adams, *The Writings of Samuel Adams*, Harry Alonzo

Cushing, editor (New York: G. P. Putnam's Sons, 1906), Vol. II, p. 351, from "The Rights Of The Colonists, A List of Violations Of Rights and A Letter Of Correspondence, Adopted by the Town of Boston, November 20, 1772," originally published in the *Boston Record Commissioners' Report*, Vol. XVIII, pp. 94-108.

[39] John Locke, *Two Treatises of Government* (London: A. Bettesworth, 1728), Book II, p. 231,Ch. XI, §134.

[40] Alexander Hamilton, John Jay, and James Madison, *The Federalist, or the New Constitution Written in 1788* (Philadelphia: Benjamin Warner, 1818), p. 281, Federalist #51 by Alexander Hamilton.

[41] Alexander Hamilton, John Jay, and James Madison, *The Federalist, or the New Constitution Written in 1788* (Philadelphia: Benjamin Warner, 1818), p. 420, Federalist #78 by Alexander Hamilton.

[42] John Locke, *Two Treatises of Government* (London: A. Bettesworth, 1728), Book II, p. 271, Ch. XVI, § 192.

[43] John Quincy Adams, *The Jubilee of the Constitution. A Discourse Delivered at the Request of the New York Historical Society, in the City of New York, on Tuesday, the 30th of April, 1839; Being the Fiftieth Anniversary of the Inauguration of George Washington as President of the United States, on Thursday, the 30th of April, 1789* (New York: Samuel Colman, 1839), p. 40.

[44] John Locke, *Two Treatises of Government* (London: A. Bettesworth, 1728), *passim.*

[45] John Adams, *The Works of John Adams*, Charles Francis Adams, editor (Boston: Little, Brown and Company, 1856), Vol. X, pp. 45-46, to Thomas Jefferson on June 28, 1813.

[46] See, for example, Richard Watson, *Theological Institutes: Or a View of the Evidences, Doctrines, Morals, and Institutions of Christianity* (New York: Carlton and Porter, 1857), Vol. I, p. 5, where Watson includes John Locke as a theologian.

[47] See, for example, *Concise Oxford Dictionary of World Religions*, John Bowker, editor (Oxford: Oxford University Press, 2000), p. 151; Franklin L. Baumer, *Religion and the Use of Skepticism* (New York: Harcourt, Brace, & Company), pp. 57-59; James A. Herrick, *The Radical Rhetoric of the English Deists: The Discourse of Skepticism, 1680-1750* (Columbia, SC: University of South Carolina Press, 1997), p. 15; Kerry S. Walters, *Rational Infidels: The American Deists* (Durango, CO: Longwood Academic, 1992), pp. 24, 210; Kerry S. Walters, *The*

American Deists: Voices of Reason and Dissent in the Early Republic (Lawrence: University Press of Kansas, 1992), pp. 6-7; John W. Yolton, *John Locke and the Way of Ideas* (Oxford: Oxford University Press, 1956), pp. 25, 115.

[48] Jack M. Balkin, "Tradition, Betrayal, and the Politics of Deconstruction – Part II," *Yale University*, 1998 (at: http://www.yale.edu/lawweb/jbalkin/articles/trad2.htm).

[49] Kyle-Anne Shiver, "Deconstructing Obama," *AmericanThinker. com*, July 28, 2008 (at: http://www.americanthinker.com/2008/07/deconstructing_obama.html).

[50] Richard Price, *Observations on the Importance of the American Revolution and the Means of Making it a Benefit to the World* (Boston: True and Weston, 1818), p. 24.

[51] Noah Webster, *An American Dictionary of the English Language* (New York: S. Converse, 1828), s.v. "infidel."

[52] James Wilson, *The Works of the Honourable James Wilson*, Bird Wilson, editor (Philadelphia: Lorenzo Press, 1804), Vol. I, pp. 67-68, "Of the General Principles of Law and Obligation."

[53] Thomas Jefferson, *The Works of Thomas Jefferson*, Paul Leicester Ford, editor (New York: G. P. Putnam's Sons, 1904), Vol. II, pp. 253-254, "Notes on Religion," October, 17

LEGEND 13

PETER FRANCISCO

VOICED BY: **GARY NEWELL**

The legend of Peter Francisco is told by Gary Newell.

(see Legend #2 for my initial introduction of Gary).

I first heard the story of Peter Francisco when Gary came to speak at Patriot Academy on "the fighting spirit." I was blown away by Francisco's amazing legend and so thankful that Gary brought it to life for us at Patriot Academy. I'm even more thankful that he brings it to life for you now in the following pages.

Peter Francisco is a Legend of Liberty whose service in the Revolutionary War was instrumental to our victory."

- Rick Green

I know what you're thinking...

Oh no... the "out of the box" guy again!

I'm back, but without a Preface this time.
I can't wait for you to get started. You're going to love this one.

The same rules still apply...

That means... read the story out loud... no arguing!

Just read the story...
ready...
begin reading...

Early summer on the island of Terceira is as beautiful as this world gets. Turquoise waters surrounded by lush hills, its simply breathtaking. Terceira is part of the Azores Islands, which are located about 950 miles from Portugal.

At the top of a hill sat a beautiful mansion overlooking the harbor of Porto Judeu. From the courtyard, the children could watch dolphins and whales jumping and playing in the ocean.

A young girl was tossing
around a ball with her little brother...
Suddenly, the boy stopped...
A curious sound caught his attention.

It sounded like the chirping of an Azores buzzard.

The lad listened...and then darted through the courtyard gate... running off to find the tropical bird.

...an action that I imagine is pretty typical...I'd love to see an Azores buzzard...
...when was the last time you saw one?

Unfortunately, he didn't find the tropical bird...

Instead...he ran into two sailors who enticed him away with candy.
(Candy was a rarity on the island, and simply too hard for him to resist.)

The last his sister saw as she chased after him were the two sailors throwing a burlap sack over her brother ...
one of the men flipped him over his shoulder...
and they ran down the hill to the harbor.

On June 23, 1765... a ship dropped anchor in the James river in Virginia.

A longboat was lowered into the water.
Two sailors rowed the boat to the wharf.

Out of the boat stepped a young boy...
...a few weeks short of his fifth birthday.

He had olive skin...
black hair...
and was noticeably big for his age.

He sat alone on the dock and watched as the sailors rowed the longboat back to the ship, boarded, and sailed out of sight over the horizon.

Old Caleb, the dock's night watchman, had just settled down in his cot for sleep when he heard what sounded like the wailing of a wounded animal.

He made his way to the end of the dock and found the wailing did not come from an animal, but from the uncontrollable sobs of a five-year-old boy.

As other dockworkers arrived they gathered around the boy. He tried to communicate with them but his words were foreign to the Virginians.

...maybe Portuguese, mixed with French...
...or maybe Spanish, they began to reason.

On his shoes were silver buckles with the initials, P.F.

He kept repeating the name,
"Pedro Francisco. Pedro Francisco."

He was promptly called "Peter" by the English colonists.

The town fathers found an unused bed for Peter,
in a dock warehouse...
...the local housewives, fed him...
...and at night, Old Caleb guarded him.

A local judge, Anthony Winston... the uncle of Patrick Henry... took the young boy in as an indentured servant.

Judge Winston was the owner of the 3,600-acre Hunting Tower Plantation. It was here that Peter began his new life, a life he never imagined before. He had his own living quarters and learned the blacksmith trade.

Peter continued to grow, by the time he was twelve-years-old he was over six feet tall and weighed 200 pounds. At the age of fifteen, he stood six-feet-six-inches tall and weighed 260 pounds.

Today, he would make a pretty good tight end in the National Football League, but to put this in perspective... at that time, the average man stood five-feet-nine-inches tall.

Peter was a young giant.

On March 23, 1775...

Judge Winston brought the fifteen-year-old Peter with him to

Richmond, Virginia for a meeting of the Virginia Convention in St. John's Church.

As an indentured servant, Peter was not allowed to enter the church. Once the delegates, including the Judge, George Washington, and Thomas Jefferson entered the building, Peter moved to the open window so he could hear Patrick Henry's speech.

Peter listened intently as Patrick Henry delivered a fiery, and what would later become famous, speech. He ended with the words...

> "Is life so dear, or peace so sweet, as to be
>   purchased at the price of chains and slavery?
>   Forbid it, Almighty God!
> I know not what course others may take; but as for me,
>   give me liberty or give me death!"

...Peter's emotions overflowed. He wanted to join the militia immediately.

Judge Winston, impressed with the young man's patriotism, told him he must wait a year, but that he would allow him to join the militia once he was sixteen-years-old.

In December 1776, at the age of sixteen, Peter Francisco enlisted as a private in the 10th Virginia Regiment.

In May 1777, he was sent to Middle Brook, New Jersey and assigned to General George Washington's Continental Army, a ragtag militia made up of some ten thousand men assembled for battle.

It was a foggy morning on September 11, 1777, near Brandywine Creek at Chad's Ford. General Washington was riding up and down the lines encouraging the colonists. Washington's men were stationed and waited as General Howe's troops marched toward them. Peter had been enlisted for over six months but had not yet been involved in battle.

That was all about to change.

As the sun began to rise in the eastern sky, musket shots rang out. General Howe's militia began to route the Continental Army. Peter's regiment took the field to halt the British advance and protect the American rear.

They stood their ground valiantly, and allowed Washington to retreat and save his army.

During the skirmish Peter felt a sharp
pain in his left leg, but ignored it.
He continued to take down every
remaining Redcoat that surrounded them.

An eerie silence fell over the battleground, as the fighting ended. Peter looked down and saw his britches soaked in blood all the way to his knee high socks. Adrenaline had kept him going, he didn't even realize the pain he felt was a musket ball going through his leg.

Peter was evacuated and sent to the home of a Moravian farmer for medical attention. While there, he met and befriended the

famous French General,
Marquis de Lafayette.

Lafayette had also been wounded and was recuperating at the same farmhouse.

Within a few short weeks Peter rejoined his regiment...
Just in time to fight in the Battle of Germantown.

On October 3rd, the 10th Virginia set out for Germantown.
A heavy fog rolled in overnight.
By morning, the soldiers could not see
more than thirty yards in front of them.

Once again, the battle was lost.

Peter's regiment stood their ground, just as they did at Brandywine, and allowed the retreating troops to get to safety.

From October to November, Peter was on duty at Mud Island. On December 19, 1777, he joined General George Washington for the long, hard winter at Valley Forge.

Some 3,000 soldiers would die at Valley Forge that winter.
...not from battle...
...but from the elements, sickness, and disease.

Peter became ill from exposure to the bitter cold.

His friend, General Lafayette came to his aid and had him transferred to the hospital at Yellow Springs.

For almost two months Peter fought, what was probably, pneumonia.

By mid-February the elixir of soup and rest worked, and he returned to Valley Forge.

His tour of duty had ended, but Peter re-enlisted. General Lafayette arranged for Peter to be assigned to him as his personal assistant.

On the morning of June 28, 1778, Peter took part in the Battle of Monmouth Courthouse. He took another musket-ball to the same thigh, but this time the ball didn't pass through the leg.

The musket-ball lodged deep in Peter's thigh, and once again he found himself in the hospital.

By October, Peter Francisco was back to soldiering.

The next year, General George Washington handpicked Peter as one of twenty soldiers to attack the British Fort at Stony Point on the Hudson River.

...Eighteen of the twenty soldiers didn't
make it out of Stony Point alive.

Peter received a nine-inch slash across his abdomen...
He grabbed his assailant, and with a fierce bear hug,
literally squeezed the life out of him.

According to some reports, despite his wound, he charged

the Fort and seized the British flag. Holding the Union Jack against his bleeding wound, he dropped to the ground, too exhausted to move...

...but his actions helped force a surrender from the Redcoats.

Two days later, Peter awoke in the hospital at West Point. Next to his bed stood Marquis de Lafayette and George Washington.

News of Peter's bravery and fame spread.

He recuperated in Fishkill, New York as his
second tour of duty came to an end...
...but Peter was not finished.

He re-enlisted for a third tour of duty.

In mid-July 1780, Peter was back with the Virginia Militia.

It was a moonless, sultry night on Tuesday, August 15, 1780, in Camden, South Carolina. The Virginia Militia marched to battle against Lord Cornwallis' army.

At dawn the following morning, Cornwallis struck first. As the Redcoats fired a volley and charged with bayonets, thousands of militiamen from North Carolina and Virginia dropped their muskets and ran.

Most had never been in battle before.

Amazingly, their general, General Horatio Gates, fled the battle on the fastest horse he could find.

Peter tried...to no avail...to rally the frightened troops.

When forced to retreat through the pinewoods, Peter saw a British grenadier raise his musket to bayonet Colonel William Mayo. Peter saved the colonel's life with a single shot.

One of the British Cavalry troopers spotted Peter and Colonel Mayo and attacked. Colonel Mayo continued his escape, while Peter faced the cavalryman.

The green-coated trooper drew his sword and ordered Peter to throw down his musket.

Peter stepped aside and as the trooper turned to cut him down, Peter swiftly bayoneted him, and toppled him from his saddle.

Peter mounted the horse...
    ...rode through the advancing British line...
        ...impersonating a Tory and yelling orders
            to the troops.

He spotted Colonel Mayo being dragged along on foot...
                    ...the prisoner of a British officer.

Peter cut the British officer down, gave the horse to Colonel Mayo, and told him to ride to safety.

Once the Colonel departed, legends record that Peter performed one of the most amazing feats of the war.

In the midst of the confusion and retreating Continental

Army, Peter spotted an abandoned small cannon attached to an artillery horse that was killed in battle.

Are you ready for this? Be sure you read this aloud...

There was no way Peter was going to allow the British to capture the American cannon. Reportedly, he loosened the gun carriage, lifted the 1,100-pound cannon onto his back and staggered towards a group of Continental soldiers.

Keep reading aloud, it gets even better...

Exhausted, he sat under a tree to regain his strength.

Peter barely caught his breath when a British trooper burst through the pines with his musket drawn and gave Peter a choice...surrender or die!

Not a good move on the part of the British soldier.

Peter appeared meek and defeated, declaring that his musket was unloaded as he surrendered it to his captor.

You know he's not going to surrender, don't you?
Listen to this...

> As the British soldier reached for the musket,
> Peter twirled it around, and thrust its
> bayonet through the trooper. He then
> mounted the dying man's horse, and in the
> confusion, galloped off, once again, impersonating
> a Redcoat, and yelling victory cheers.

You've got to admit, that would make for a great movie! So after the defeat at Camden, Peter returned to Virginia.

He learned that Captain Thomas Watkins planned to put a unit in the field, so on January 17, 1781, Peter returned to South Carolina to face the Legion of Banastre Tarleton, at the Battle of Cowpens.

The guy doesn't know how to quit. Amazing!

After the Battle of Cowpens, Peter became the personal aide of Lt. Colonel William Washington, the second cousin of George Washington. The Lt. Colonel took his cavalry troop south to join forces with General Nathaniel Greene in North Carolina.

It was at this time that another great Francisco legend surfaced. Reportedly, Peter had been complaining about the sword he had been using because it was more like a toothpick in his hands than an effective weapon.

The story goes on to report that on March 13, 1781, a supply wagon sent from George Washington, arrived at General Greene's camp. Among the food and clothing was a crate addressed to Lt. Colonel William Washington. In the crate was a gift for Peter Francisco...

General George Washington gave special orders to have a broadsword forged for Peter. It was six-feet long with a five-foot blade.

Now we have America's version of William Wallace!

The broadsword came just in time...

Two days later, on the bright, crisp afternoon of March 15th, General Cornwallis' British infantry moved up the slope around the Guilford Courthouse.

General Greene's first and second lines opened fire on the Redcoats, and drove them back in retreat.

Cornwallis had his infantry regroup and mount a bayonet charge that breached the heart of Greene's frontline. The Continentals ran for the woods in fear.

However, the second line of Greene's army was a defiant group.

An American bugler sounded the charge and Lt. Colonel Washington's cavalrymen, including Peter, rushed down the wooded slope. The battle was intense and Peter fought valiantly with his massive broadsword.

One British grenadier drove his bayonet into Peter's right thigh and pinned it to the horse. The whole length of the bayonet entered above the knee and came out at the socket of his hip.

I'd say that made Peter rather angry...

So much so, that with powerful force, he brought down his broadsword and split his assailant's head, all the way to his shoulders.

Do I really need to explain that?
I think you've got the picture.

Peter rode his horse a short distance and fell from his saddle, unconscious.

As John Robinson, a local Quaker, later walked the battlefield in search of survivors, he found Peter beside four corpses. Several men lifted him onto a wagon and brought him to the Robinson's farm.

Martha Robinson nursed the giant soldier back to health. After six to eight weeks, Peter said goodbye to the Robinson family and walked 200 miles back to Virginia.

...Yes, the man walked home...it took weeks, but the man walked home.

Even after his fourth injury, Peter still had some soldiering left in him.

Finally back home, Peter was on a trip to town and stopped to take a break at Ben Ward's Tavern in the Nottoway County village of Amelia. While he sat quietly at the inn, a party of nine of Tarleton's Dragoons galloped up to the tavern.

Peter tried to escape but was surrounded. He had no weapon so he lifted his hands and surrendered.

Eight of the Dragoons went into the tavern leaving one trooper to guard Peter. The soldier ordered Peter to empty his pockets hoping to find something of value. Peter had nothing valuable in his possession.

The Dragoon spotted two shining shoe buckles with the letters P.F.. He demanded Peter to hand over the buckles.

Big mistake...

Peter told him that he wouldn't hand them over...they were very special to him... But if he wanted them, he could come take them himself.

The trooper tucked his sword under his arm and bent down to take the buckles.

Bigger mistake...

Peter took a step backward, grabbed the sword, and in one swift motion he slashed the Dragoon's head and neck.

The soldier managed a last, desperate, cry for help, which alerted the other eight troopers inside. As they ran out of the Tavern, they encountered an armed giant... Peter Francisco.

By the time the fight ended, Peter struck
down a second Dragoon...
...Seven others ran for their lives...

...and Peter was left with eight horses for himself.

The stories and legends of Peter Francisco continue to endure over the decades. Some may be more exaggerated than others... we have no way of knowing.

Peter is known as "the Hercules of the American Revolution..."
a "one man army..."
"the Virginia Giant..."
and even, the "greatest soldier in American history."

Many popular histories of Francisco's life record a statement by George Washington that says, "Without [Francisco] we would have lost two crucial battles, perhaps the war, and with it our freedom."

The origin of the quote is unknown. However, Peter's documented battle record, multiple enlistments, and wounds inspire amazement all by themselves.

An orphan.
An indentured servant.
An enlisted soldier.
An unwavering Patriot.

An American hero...

A champion. A winner!

Peter Francisco was the embodiment of the "Fighting Spirit."

The "Fighting Spirit" is paramount to winning in life.

Please allow me to conclude with three simple characteristics of the "Fighting Spirit." These three characteristics are readily seen in Peter, and can be found in virtually every champion.

...by the way...you can stop reading out loud now.

You're almost done. Just three short thoughts...

The "Fighting Spirit" is identified in the...

<u>HEART</u> of the Winner...
<u>ATTITUDE</u> of the Winner...
<u>PASSION</u> of the Winner...

A Winner's <u>HEART</u> must be a warrior's heart.

A warrior's heart is simply the ability to keep getting up when you get knocked down. Peter showed this heart his entire career.

Today, most people never really win because they fail to fail enough. All great success is based on failure.

The challenges we face make life interesting...
But overcoming them makes life meaningful.

It takes a warrior's heart.

A warrior never allows his challenges to push him around. Rather, he chooses to be led by his dreams. Turning challenges into opportunities and defeats into victories is a requirement for the warrior.

The masses never really win because they fear failing more than they desire winning.

Losers quit when they're tired. Winners quit when they've won.

Peter Francisco only knew how to win. He had a warrior's heart.

A Winner's ATTITUDE is the beginning of winning.

To say that attitude is everything, is an understatement. Attitude is that one determining factor of whether our failures make or break us.

I love Peter Francisco's attitude. He simply refused to break.

Attitudes are a choice.
Choose wisely... you become either the master or the victim of your attitude.

It's our attitude that determines our winning. Those attitudes begin with our thoughts. Whatever thoughts hold our attention, also determines our actions. In reality, our attitude is as simple as our habits of thought.

In his book, "*The Winning Attitude*," author, speaker, and friend, John Maxwell, says that our attitude is the primary force that will determine whether we succeed or fail. He gives seven important Attitude Axiom's concerning our attitude. They are:

1 Our attitude determines our approach to life.

2 Our attitude determines our relationship with people.

3 Often our attitude is the only difference between success and failure.

4 Our attitude at the beginning of a task will affect its outcome more than anything else.

5 Our attitude can turn our problems into blessings.

6 Our attitude can give us an uncommonly positive perspective.

7 Our attitude is not automatically good just because we are Christians.

That book, as with all of John Maxwell's books, is an excellent source for creating a Winning ATTITUDE...

and to think... Peter Francisco couldn't even read.

I'm extremely thankful for John Maxwell's friendship and mentorship over the last two decades...it changed my attitude...

...so how's that for props, John!

It's obvious... attitude is imperative to winning!

A Winner's PASSION is the fuel that keeps you going.

It's passion that will keep you going when you face those obstacles, setbacks, failures, fears, and doubts.

Passion drives your dreams and goals.

Passion fuels you with energy...
...and without energy, you're out of gas.

It's okay to be a little fanatical about winning in life... about chasing your dreams... about making a difference.

It's okay to love what you do so much that you can't wait for another day so you can get up and do it all over again.

That's the passion that fuels the winner.

In 1829, the "Petition of Peter Francisco," which he penned in 1820, was read to the General Assembly of Congress. In it, he wrote...

> ...that he "never felt satisfied, nor thought he did a good day's work, but by drawing British blood."

That may not be politically correct by today's standards, but you've go to admit, the man was passionate!

> While sitting under an open window at the
> Old North Church...
> listening to Patrick Henry...
> ...a "Fighting Spirit" was birthed in the
> heart of a fifteen year old indentured servant.

The cause for freedom imparted the heart, attitude, and passion that inspired Peter Francisco to join a rag-tag Continental Army of volunteers, that never once had an army of over 15,000 troops, and yet, defeated the most powerful military force in the world.

Sadly, too many today have substituted passion for pleasure.

I leave you with the sobering words from one of this country's most prominent and passionate Founding Fathers, Samuel Adams...

"If you love wealth greater than liberty, the tranquility of servitude greater than the animating contest for freedom, go home from us in peace. We seek not your counsel, nor your arms. Crouch down and lick the hand that feeds you; May your chains set lightly upon you, and may posterity forget that you were our countrymen."

Wow... the power of passion is not always popular!

My prayer is that this story of Peter Francisco sparks in you the boldness to find that one thing you are passionate about...

...that one thing you can chase with all of your "Fighting Spirit..."

...that one thing that will make a difference in our world, and fulfill your true destiny.

LEGEND 14

SUJO JOHN

VOICED
BY:
**KRISH
DHANAM**

The legend of Sujo John is told by my friend, Krish Dhanam.

A more formal introduction of Krish is included the introduction of Legend #5, Zig Ziglar, also contributed by Krish.

Given the opportunity for a second introduction of Krish, I'd like to share a personal note about him. Our friendship goes far enough back that he was part of a small group of friends at the weekend retreat where I proposed to Kara. Twenty-one years later, just weeks after the release of this book, Krish will help officiate the wedding ceremony of my son, Trey (voice of Legend #6), and his bride-to-be, Alexandra Murphy (voice of Legend #10).

Krish is one of those rare individuals who always lifts your spirit and makes you want to be a better person. He has been the highest rated speaker at Patriot Academy for five years in a row. I'm convinced he is the favorite of the students not just because of his unmatched speaking abilities, but because of the personal investment he makes in conversation with the students at meals and breaks.

Very simply, Krish Dhanam cares about the success of other people and he has spent his life mastering practical, golden nuggets of wisdom to consistently sow into those blessed enough to cross his path.

When I first read the legend you are about to read, it became obvious to me that Sujo John, like Krish, uses his story and the wisdom he has learned to improve the lives of other people. Sujo John is a legend of liberty whose miraculous story became a testimony of inspiration to people all over the world.

- Rick Green

Sujo John
An Ember for Change

"The way to love anything is to realize that it may be lost."
- G. K. Chesterton

Lady Liberty stands guard in the harbor and the words etched into her on a plaque remind an immigrant of the world that was and the one that now is. Sitting in his office in the World Trade Towers, he glances at his watch to get ready for the day and to remind himself of his good fortune. He decides to write an e-mail to a friend a little before 8:00 AM on the 11th of September, 2011. The contents of the email are more a query about life, purpose and possibility. The contents of life are more vivid--a young bride (carrying their first child) who works in the other tower in the same complex. A boy raised in a far-off city that was made famous by Mother Teresa would soon come to grips with a destiny that would alter his life. Ignorance and evil would unleash hell on an unsuspecting populace, and through the burnt embers of carnage and mayhem, God would place His hand on the life of Sujo John and offer a miracle.

They say the American Dream is rooted in the want for new

beginnings and the desire for a level playing field where anyone can make it. Since the shots heard at Concord and Lexington, a fledgling republic shaped itself as the last beacon of freedom and the only hope for millions who wanted a chance at a better life. Sujo was no different, as he emigrated from India to America in search of life and liberty. There he sat, counting his blessings, looking at a statue that had beckoned millions before him. Life was good, but the need for meaning was gnawing at him in a profound way. Little did he know what lay ahead in the immediate moments that followed. Who amongst us will not remember the tragic events of 9/11/2001? Better yet, who amongst us has the courage to forget the cowardice of a band of thugs who altered the landscape of a nation and, through it, the world? 9/11 is often only remembered as numbers by historians but relived as a dark memory by Sujo John, who crawled his way down flights of stairs and scraped his way through fallen rubble. 9/11 was a day when the world changed for some and a new world was born for others.

When you see lightning you are almost always ready for thunder. When you hear a loud explosion you always look towards the window if you are inside to see if you can patch together what happened. What if the sound is the loudest you have ever heard, the building you are in begins to shake, there is a gigantic hole where your roof used to be, and there is paper flying everywhere as the window is broken? What would you do next? Some think of their own mortality and your life passes you by in slow motion, frame by frame. What if your life is just beginning and you are young with hopes, dreams and aspirations? That was the moment Sujo John knew that he knew. In the immediate dark moments that were filled with smoke and smelled of burnt flesh, all Sujo could think of was his bride and the child she was carrying. Two explosions, two planes, two buildings and destruction as far as the eye could see. Airplane fuel is the tinder that is melting steel and a gaping hole ten floors deep is the reminder that something unprecedented has just happened. For those of us gripped to our television sets across the globe, we saw the tears of reporters as they were unable to describe the apocalyptic images. Cameramen had to turn their cameras away to avoid capturing images of muffled screams and flailing arms, as people jumped to their death from 80 floors above. Inside this cage of utter pandemonium, God was preparing the life of Sujo John to become His chosen emissary to the world. A young man at the prime of his life and the beginning of his career in finance--in the very place that shouts bulls and bears-- would be brought to grips with an unfathomable reality. Like Paul, he would hurt and be blinded, but when his eyes opened he would see clearly why he had been chosen for America. He would be spared, but not before his eyes had seen the depths of depravity that humanity is capable of. He would become believable when he gave a helping hand. One wise man said that in order to lift someone up you must first be on higher ground. When Sujo speaks of American exceptionalism in the form of the FBI and the NYPD, he has earned the right. To be able to talk about love in the decades to follow he would have to first consume the precept of hate as it was unfurled all around him. Like patriots of old, his number would be called. The experience of the calling so direct. The aftermath of the horror so recent.

He saw the first responders race up the stairs, knowing that the flames he left on his way down would consume them. Their bravery continues to inspire him to always be able to run towards the dangers that confront others. When the buildings around began to tremble and the ground below began to shake, he knew that what was about to ensue may be the beginning of the journey that would let him meet his Lord. He quickly gathered people in a huddle and told them to accept Christ as their Savior. Some did meet Him that day and only because one man thought that heaven needed a party as one repented amidst hell on earth. In the dust and the fog caused by debris all around, he gasped for air. A sound and a light alerted him, and he moved towards the tones of rescue. A man beckoned for and then dragged Sujo to safety and then returned to the rubble to help another. The man who had helped him to live did not get to save himself and died. Such moments define you and give you a resilience to face whatever life throws at you.

The hours dragged along as he wondered what the future held. He stared at the wall of ruins as two monolithic buildings reduced to metal and concrete separated him from anything and everything he knew. Lamenting on the sidewalk with no cellular reception caused the silence for the remainder of that day. A silence that would grow in reflection and groan in agony. Why me, God? Is my bride alive? What about my unborn child? Give her back to me in any condition and I will care for her. Spare her Lord. Spare my child. Please Father. I will give my life to You and serve You.

Similar prayers were being said on a sidewalk on the other side of the rubble by his beloved. His bride had not made it up to the top of her building, as she had missed her train and the attacks had already begun by the time she had gotten there. She had spent a day asking the same questions and dealing with the same doubt. Spare him, Lord. Give him back to me in any condition and I will serve You all the days of my life. Father,

Father please! Then as dusk settles and the numbed senses begin awakening to the reality of the aftermath--a miracle. God answers. The cell phone rings. It's his beloved Mary. Are you okay? I Love you. So good to hear your voice. I thought you were... Don't cry. It will be all right. I will see you soon. I love you.

Once reunited and quarantined and back in the confines of their abode, Sujo and Mary get down on their knees and commission their lives to the Gospel of Jesus Christ. They did not know the trajectory of the future and why they had been put to this test. They could not conceive the uncertainty of followership. They only knew that everything would be different and they were ready. They had been tried and tested and saved for a purpose.

A speaking and proclamation ministry is born. From the humble altars of churches in rural America, to the halls of corporations and political houses, to the very nation that sent the people who unleashed the horror of the day that changed his life, Sujo John has become a modern-day American legend. As a motivational speaker, proclamation evangelist, and spokesperson for the destitute, he has articulated with eloquence and clarity the reason why he was spared. In an age when correctness of vocabulary is designed to not be provocative, he uses the imagery of 9/11 to depict evil and then shows faith and love through example. He takes the embers of burnt dreams and incinerated hopes and weaves a fabric of responsibility that can become a shroud of optimism to those that call this land of the free home. From preaching the saving grace of his Savior to starting a foundation to rescue those trafficked in human dignity, this modern-day Wilberforce is a true hero of epic proportions. Day after day, week after week, and month after month, he has tirelessly carried this burden to nations across the globe. While his causation is human, and the restoration of dignity a calling, he understands that there can be no calling without a caller. Sujo John is and always will be the epitome of the American Dream.

The words of Alexis de Tocqueville are a subtle reminder of the resilience of the spirit of people who call this great nation home. A humble immigrant with the heart of a lion confronts the tragedy of the moment and refuses to become a victim of circumstance, but instead becomes a champion of the downtrodden and destitute. He takes the putrid smoke and pungent odor of hopelessness and converts that into the sweet incense of love and forgiveness. He harbors no hatred for those that caused architectural ruin and prays for redemption for them. He lives the Christ -like motto of loving his enemies. He brings to mind the militiamen who took on the mighty powers of imperial supremacy and fought because that was the only option left. When Sujo had his 9/11, he was destined to be the one that forced a new shot to be heard around the world.

The lessons he teaches are profound in their application and diverse in their reach. When he is confronted by the controversy of his faith he stands even more firm in the pursuit of his dreams. The images from 9/11 will haunt us all for the rest of our natural lives. We saw a presidency defined by it, a nation thrust into war because of it, and a deep divide in humanity created because of it. Geography was forever settled by terms that became directional and East and West had to contend with the Middle. Negotiation was called weak and torture extreme. If you lost your head in a debate you were labeled bigoted and made the news for a week. If you happened to be beheaded because someone wanted it so, then you were circulated in a video with a title that said "too graphic." Amidst the chaos of life moving on and society coping with evil as a necessary addition to civility, Sujo John remains focused. When you hear him speak you will know he loves his God. When you see him live you will know he loves his country. When you relive his moments you will know why God spared him that fateful day. God bless you, Sujo, for your example. God bless Mary and the children for their faithfulness, and God bless America.

LEGEND

15

KING DAVID

VOICED
BY:

CLIFF GRAHAM

The legend of King David is told by one of my favorite authors, Cliff Graham.

Cliff is a speaker, writer and former Army soldier and officer. He is the author of the *Lion of War* series and the *Shadow of the Mountain* series. Conceived as gritty, intense, and exciting novels that would help a new generation connect with the Bible, Cliff's ability to bring the stories of King David and his Mighty Men to life is unparalleled. *Day of War*, his first novel, will soon be an epic film. I highly recommend his entire series for mature readers, but with a warning. Cliff's books are extremely violent. However, they are no more violent than Scripture itself—just more violent than many previous novels based on Scripture. His novels also contain mature themes of sexual temptation and lust that demand that readers be mature enough to understand them. Please exercise caution and discretion.

The legend of King David told by Cliff here is gritty, but does not address the mature themes listed above. This chapter is a direct excerpt from Cliff's *Hall of the Mighty Men*.

King David is included as one of our Legend's of Liberty because he fought to free his people from the barbarism of Israel's enemies, while also writing the Psalms that help so many of us find true liberty in the same God David served.

- Rick Green

A note from the author -- "This book is intended to be accurate to the time of its setting, but it is fiction. Many modern terms and phrases are used in dialog, and to describe military units, actions, and cultural aspects that will be easily understood and accessible to the modern reader.

Some aspects of chronology and characterization are products of the author's imagination."

"IN HONOR OF THE TENTH YEAR OF SOLOMON, son of David, the beloved of the Lord, king in Jerusalem, I have been commissioned to record the chronicles of those warriors known as the Mighty Men for you, great king. They were the men who came to your father in his hour of need. They were the men who fought with him. They were men, and that is the highest that can be written of them.

I, Jehoshaphat, recorder of the court of Solomon the Wise, saw these men. I spoke to them. I heard their souls. I testify to their courage in the days when the people of Israel had none.

Are not their deeds recorded in the histories, composed by the prophet's chroniclers? Surely those books shall last through time.

My purpose here is to tell the tales of unknown times in their lives. Perhaps it will strengthen those who now live in the Hall of the Mighty Men. Perhaps it will remind aspiring men that even the heroes had their beginnings. But surely it will remind you of your legacy, great king, and the cost of your kingdom.

None of these great men I shall chronicle would have suffered my embellishments of their character, much as I would be tempted.

Instead, as the noble Shammah once told me, ensure that praise is given to our God.

I shall do so, and in the course of giving praise to our God, may these tales of brave warriors who knew the covering be arrows to his enemies."

(For stories of Benaiah, Ittai, Eliahba, Ira, Gareb and more Mighty Men, get Cliff Graham's "The Hall of the Mighty Men" at CliffGraham.com. Cliff has graciously shared his chapter on David as our Legend of Liberty #15 and we pick up the story there...)

We turn now to your father, the greatest of all the champions. He was first among them in skill and esteem. But what has he told you of his childhood? The tales of his battlefield bravery are known to many, but he always claimed that Yahweh molded him into a king when he was in the wild lands as a youth, protecting his father's flocks.

He has gone to Sheol now. His sling has stilled forever. It will, regretfully, never crush another Philistine skull. But every man's time for that journey eventually comes. As does mine.

I came to him near the end, when he was old and being comforted by the young woman who kept his bed warm. He told me that it was urgent that I bring my writing properties at once to his bedside. As I stepped into his bedchamber in the palace, I could make him out in the light of the dim oil lamp. The young woman was not there, he must have sent her elsewhere for this meeting.

The great king was old, his hair grey and body tremulous. He was covered in robes and blankets to stay warm.

As I sat at his feet, he began to tell me of his childhood and youth, and I recorded them. Many stories. Perhaps I will be able to write them all out at a later time, but it was one story in particular that he seemed to wish I record for you, and which I now present.

Your father had many layers of his heart and soul. The infamy of his treachery and betrayal of his men never left him, and broke him late in life. But that is not how he must be remembered. For when we look back to his finer days, we see a glimpse of Yahweh himself.

———————————

Imagine, oh king, a hillside in the country near Bethlehem, and a young man who lays on a rock in the sun.

Sheep bleat lazily in the meadow around him. Insects hover around his ears and he swats at them passively.

He is lost in thought. A melody emanates from his lips, then he mutters something to the tune of it. He shakes his head, not satisfied. He brings up the melody again, only this time changing the words around.

It seems to work, and he nods to himself. His lips part in a broad grin, and now he sits up, singing full-throated. His voice is clear and powerful. A sheep nearby turns and faces him, chewing slowly.

David stares directly at the sheep's eyes and sings the refrain again.

> *"The Lord is my shepherd; I shall not want.*
> *He makes me lie down in green pastures.*
> *He leads me beside still waters.*
> *He restores my soul."*

David nods to himself, satisfied. It would all come together, in time. The full song.

"I will convince you of his majesty, Speckle Leg, if it is the final act of my life."

Speckle Leg was given his name because of the dusting of black fur mixed in with the gray on his hindquarters. David knows every one of these sheep and has given them all names. Some are named after his brothers, though he does not tell them this. They contend with him enough as it is.

David sings the song again, forcing his voice to echo around the meadow. The sheep continue eating, used to this display.

The song ends. David closes his eyes, feeling the sunlight warm his face. The smell of spring everywhere. Water trickling from the creek in the woods. Grass between his toes. Yahweh has provided all of it, and he is grateful.

"Lord, I wonder at it. Wonder at how you could have mercy on someone like me. How you make things new every morning," David says, standing to stretch his legs. "Every day is gift. Every day is gift."

For what must be the tenth time that day, he thinks back to the prophet's visit. There was a warmth in his chest, a pain that came over him from his eyes to his toes, and he felt as though his heart would burst from unimaginable fire. The sound of the voice of Yahweh, like a lion in the darkness. The image burns in his eyes. Every time he closes them at night, he sees it. It rages at him in his dreams. Fire and pain.

But he is not dreaming now. It is only a spring afternoon, growing hotter. He will need to get the sheep into the forest soon to cool them off.

He puts his fingers to his mouth and gives the shrill whistle that the sheep recognize as his. They bunch up in the meadow and crowd their way towards him, tripping over each other's legs and hooves. He chuckles watching them.

They file one by one onto the forest game trail that leads to the cold water of the creek. Happily, he sees that none of them tries to wander away. The last one in is Speckle Leg. David picks up his staff, ensures that the sling is still tucked in his belt, and begins to follow them.

"You are to be tested."

David tenses. His eyes dart wildly from side to side, searching for the source of the voice.

"Who is there?"

He does not know why, but it seems like the voice came from the shadows under the great terebinth tree nearby. David glances at his sheep, then moves slowly towards the tree.

As he approaches, he is forced to squint in the sunlight. He cannot see past the low-hanging branches with glittering leaves. At the edge of the tree's canopy, he hesitates.

"Come inside," the voice says again.

David steadies his breathing and pushes aside the branches. When his eyes adjust to the shadows, he sees a large man standing near the trunk of the tree. He is dressed for battle. Greaves cover his legs, a breastplate on his chest. A great sword at his belt. His face is harsh.

"You are to be tested," the warrior says again.

"Who are you?"

"I serve in the armies of the Lord Most High. The Lord who

has anointed you to serve his people."

David kneels down.

"Stand. I am not him."

David rises back to his feet, allowing himself to look carefully at the man's face. He looks no different than an ordinary man, although he is large, easily a head and a half taller than himself. He appears to have scars on his neck.

"What will the Lord of my fathers have me do?"

"He desires that you trust him."

"I trust him."

"You will find out soon."

David's voice grows steadier. "What am I to face?"

The warrior seems to be appraising him, and David stiffens his back. He is confused, but he keeps his eyes locked on the warrior.

"Your life will be one of battle. You will know it all of your days. Your adversaries will prowl Yahweh's lands like lions. By the sword you will deliver Yahweh's people. By the sword you will establish peace for your son."

David feels deep truth in his words. Truth that penetrates into his soul and warms his chest. "Peace...for my son. But not for me?"

"A man's life is an offering to Yahweh. Nothing more. Nothing less. If Yahweh decrees that you shall be consumed, so be it. If he decrees that you are to be triumphant, so be that."

"And which of those will I be?"

The warrior's mouth turns up in a slight grin. "You will know Yahweh, young king. That is enough."

David waits for more, but the warrior only nods his head and steps around the side of the tree, vanishing.

David waits, tense.

"I am ready, holy God of my people, for however you would test me." What is he ready for? He does not know. Tested? David stands in place, afraid to move.

This is your first day of war. But do not fear. I shall be with you.

David searches the tree line, the meadow, all around him. No one is there. This voice is not audible. He more feels it than hears it.

And somehow, perhaps deep within his spirit, he knows what is coming. That a battle must occur, a challenge met. It shall be him against the enemy, to the glory of the Lord Most High.

The hot afternoon sun betrays no sign of danger. He holds his staff in front him and pulls the sling out of his belt. He will be ready. For what, he does not know, but he will be ready.

Speckle Leg is the last one into the tree line. David watches him, eyes alert, ears wary. The sheep are bleating now, ahead in the forest where he cannot see them. He feels panic rising. Danger. Get to the sheep.

A deafening roar, raw and powerful, from somewhere nearby.

David has the staff up in front of him. It is too close to use the sling. He checks for the flint dagger with a shaky hand. It is still there. He rushes out from under the canopy and back onto the game trail.

The roar comes again.

It come from the front of the line, where the lead sheep is following the game path to the water. There is thrashing in the bushes, an unseen force is tearing through the branches, the roaring picks up, louder. David crouches, the staff up, unable to move, terror in his heart.

A lamb shrieks. It rouses David from his stupor. A baby. An innocent.

He does not know what it is, where it is, or what he will do when he gets to it, but whatever it is is about to kill his sheep.

David pushes through the game trail crowded with sheep, pushing away the limbs, forcing his way to where he can see what is attacking them. He turns a corner and sees it.

A bear.

It is black as night, awash in the smell of gore and roaring. It bites at a lamb, and the bleating animal dangles in its mouth.

The lamb had been born only weeks ago. It still wobbles awkwardly as it walks. David loves watching it in the meadow. But now it hangs from the jaws of death. He has not even had a chance to name it yet.

David rushes forward. The bear shakes its head and tosses the lamb aside to face him. David swings the staff at the black form, striking it on the neck. It swipes a paw at him, and then David is leaping to a low-hanging branch, catching it and pulling himself up and out of reach of the bear.

The sheep are bleating in terror and crashing through the woods. David waits for the bear to pass below him, then drops onto its back. He reaches around the animal's neck with his staff and pulls it tight.

It is a monster, a force of strength greater than David can comprehend. He clamps his eyes shut and squeezes as hard as he can, his muscles burning with effort.

The bear whirls around, smashing him against the bushes. It rolls over onto its back, crushing him against the rocks. David cries out, keeps his hands frozen to the staff.

Muscle ripples in the animal's back as it thrashes around,

trying to reach David with its paws. The claws rake across his arms, cutting flesh.

David gags as the bear's scent floods his senses, the animal's spinning making him queasy. He turns his head to the side and vomits.

The bear rolls forward, and David is forced to release his grip to avoid being dashed against a boulder. He lands and then crawls behind a tree. Blood covers his face.

The bear charges the tree.

"Yahweh!" is all he can cry.

He is reacting before he even thinks it, and his arm swings the crook of the staff directly at the bear's face as it approaches, hitting the snout and making the bear howl.

I am with you.

Something like fire pours out of David's heart. He feels his arms strengthen, his courage fill. His mind sees every weakness, every area to exploit in his adversary.

The animal tries to rush him, but David is too fast. He scrambles to the side as the bear charges, jumping on his back once more.

He snakes an arm around the bear's throat, knowing it should be impossible but feeling the strength to choke the animal. The bear's muscles feel softer to him, his own body hard like stone, power immeasurable flowing into his attack. He crushes the throat of the bear between his forearm and upper arm.

The bear's roars have turned to howling. It struggles to breathe more and more, until finally it lays still.

Another roar, loud and resonant, from across the field.

David looks up and searches for the source.

A male lion, a black mane covering his shoulders, is charging across the meadow. It is roaring like the thunder of the spring storms.

But David is ready. He is not gripped by fear as he was with the bear.

"Yes, come to me!" he taunts the lion as it charges. "Come to me and I will show you might! I will show you power!"

The lion releases a long, bellowing roar that sends the sheep scurrying in all directions.

David strides forward, directly towards the lion, his pace quickening with anger and deadly purpose.

"Come to me and I will show you there is a God in Israel! And these stones too shall know it!"

David beats his chest and yells his war cry, reaching into his belt and removing his sling. He bends over to grab a stone as he runs, drops it in the pocket, and whirls it around his head.

Swing.

Measure.

Aim.

The steps of the attack repeat, he cries out in fury, feeling Yahweh's power come over him, rage unknowable.

Swing.

Measure.

Aim.

He releases the sling and the stone soars ahead of him, striking the lion in the snout. It snarls and paws at its face, and then David is upon it. He hits it on the head with all of his might and continues running. It swipes a paw and lashes his leg with hooked claws as he passes it.

David realizes in a moment that this will be more difficult than the bear. The lion is faster, has coiled strength built for running, and it chases him now.

David pounds his bare feet as fast as he can, then, without looking backwards, leaps to his left. The lion rushes past where he had been. David is agile, his legs powerful, and he races back in the direction he has just come from.

It takes several counts for the lion to slow its bulk to a stop, then turn and pick up speed for the pursuit again. David has an advantage of fifty paces.

He stops, turns, and takes the time to open his belt pouch and pull out one of his precious copper pellets. Perfectly smooth and able to be hurled with the most accuracy and force, unlike unreliable field rocks.

David drops the pellet into the sling, whirls it hard over his head three times, sees the lion charging, feels its hate as it bears down on him, and releases the pellet.

This time it strikes the creature's eye in a burst of blood and flesh. The lion roars louder but does not slow down. David crouches, waits for it to leap at him, and when it does, he rolls to his side.

The lion rushes past him again. David pulls out another pellet, loads the sling, and slings the pellet at the lion. It strikes its jaw as it turns around, adding to the blood already pouring from its eye and snout.

David knows he cannot kill the animal in this fashion, but his attacks have wounded it. The last pellet has broken away the fangs on the right side of its jaws.

He tucks the sling back into his belt and tosses his staff back into his right hand.

"That all may know of Yahweh!" he screams. "That we may be witnesses to his power!"

The lion crouches, roaring, and fire erupts all around David's vision.

He sees the heavens open up to a great scene of wars and battles that have been fought, and are yet to be fought, and he himself leading them, being bled by the wounds of many blows.

The warrior from the forest is there, his sword raised high, and he points to David with it, then to the crouched lion.

"Strike it down in the name of the Lord Most High," he says.

David yells from the depths of his lungs, the mightiest war cry he can muster, and his blood burns like flame.

He rushes forward, the lion snarls and charges, and they meet.

David puts the staff between the animal's jaws and twists his body down, using the force of the lion's leap to smashes it against the rocks nearby. The paws swipe at him, the creature snarls and roars, but David is too strong, the spirit of the Lord raging inside of him, and he is able to climb on the back as he did with the bear and choke the neck with his staff.

David holds tight as the lion thrashes about. He feels pain, but it is good pain, the pain of battle and rage, of a fight well fought, and he finds himself singing. Why does he sing? He does not know, only that Yahweh wishes him to sing, and to cry out in worship.

"My shield in dark places! My strength when I am alone!"

The lyrics are spat through blood and sweat. He winces as a claw slashes his forearm, then sings louder.

"You prepare me a table before my enemies!"

The lion starts to run across the field with David on its back, charging towards his sheep. David squeezes tighter.

"You have anointed me with oil! My cup overflows! Surely your goodness will follow me!"

The lion is closing in on the first sheep of the herd. David no longer sees the vision of the wars in heaven, but knows Yahweh is there. He feels his power, feels the protection of his warriors.

"My Lord and king! Pour me out as an offering to yourself!"

The lion lashes out at the sheep. David rolls off the beast's back and swings the staff with all of his might. It cracks against the bones of the spine, staggering it.

David presses in, his song sounding more like a scream now, and shoves his arm into the animal's throat where the jaws were broken by his pellet.

He climbs back on the animal's neck, avoiding the brutal claws.

The fire rages in his muscles one last, desperate time and he jerks the jaws to the side as hard as he can.

There is a crack like a flash of lightning, and the animal goes still immediately.

David stands, gasping for breath, covered in blood, battle rage coursing through his body.

More roaring now, across the field. From out of the woods comes another bear and another lion, running side by side.

I will give unto you battle, many enemies, and you shall strike them down in my name.

Both predators charge into the herd.

David runs forward without pausing or thinking, his feet flying over the rocky field. The bear and the lion turn and snarl at him, each with a struggling sheep in its jaws, the faces of evil. One of the sheep, struggling in the mouth of the bear, is Speckle Leg. The other is a sheep David has named Cedar.

David races through his flock, dropping a pellet into the sling and then pulling the dagger out with his free hand. He starts to whirl the sling.

The lion turns and flees in the direction of the forest where it had come. The bear does the same, although it veers off in a different direction.

The dry, hot dust makes David cough as he runs. His throat is parched, his body raging with pain and fury and strength. He must choose between them. Which one to save? The lion is fleeing into a dense stand of trees that David knows ends at the edge of a cliff. He will be able to catch it sooner. The bear is making towards a hill in the distance. First the lion, then the bear, David realizes.

It is heartrending to make the choice, but he cries out, "Do not fear, Speckle Leg! I will come to you as soon as I have saved the other one!"

Somehow he is fast enough to catch the lion as it enters the forest.

The temptation is to believe, oh king, that a man is not capable of running down a lion on his own feet. Those who would succumb to that temptation do not know the covering, and they most certainly did not know your father.

David hurls the pellet as hard as he can. It strikes the lion in the tender spot between its hind legs. The shot makes it stumble in pain but it continues forward, the bleating sheep thrashing. David knows the cliff is only strides ahead, the lion will be forced to stop.

The bramble clears, the cliff top emerges, and the lion pivots immediately from its path and to the right. David has been anticipating this move, and when the lion turns, he dives for the head with his dagger.

The tip of the blade scrapes the animal's skull, cutting a gash in its face the length of David's hand. David collides with the sheep in its mouth. The animal is thrown aside as the lion releases it to bite David.

David catches the jaws and wrenches the beard aside, exhilarated at his new strength. He stabs at the eye with his dagger until it finally pierces the socket.

The lion whips its head from side to side, the fight now gone from it, trying to free itself from David. But David holds on and continues to wrench at the head, his hands gripping the blade-like fangs, until a burst of strength in his arms allows him to snap the neck.

The beast dies. David shoves the carcass aside and looks for the sheep.

It is bleating in terror nearby. David jumps to his feet fast, his heart still pounding, and runs for the sheep. But the sudden movement spooks the animal and it turns and runs straight for the cliff. "Stop!" David shouts, fear gripping him, but he realizes too late that he will not be able to stop the animal before it leaps to its own doom.

"Yahweh, help me!"

David dives for the legs, desperate the catch it. The sheep sees the edge of the cliff and tries to turn, but it is too late. The dirty white body plunges over the side.

David slides to a stop, screaming in anguish. The sheep named Cedar tumbles several times through the air until it strikes the rocks a hundred cubits below.

David stares at the broken, crumpled form, tears stinging his eyes. He feels as though his soul has been torn from his chest.

Why did Yahweh not help him?

But there is no time to grieve, no time to waste, for he must hurry. Speckle Leg is still in the mouth of the bear.

David gets up and starts to run in the direction that he saw the bear fleeing, but then he stops. Should he go after it? Should he go back to the others? What if there are more lions and bears?

Though grief for the dead sheep is wracking his body and mind, David says aloud, "Lord, God of my salvation, where should I go?"

David feels the answer immediately.

You shall pursue the lone sheep, for that is how I pursue you.

"Thank you, great Father. Though you crush me, I hear and obey."

The fire in his body flares up again, as though a dry log has been thrown on coals, and David runs with the fleetness of the deer through the forest.

As he runs, his sorrow for the dead sheep turns to anger. How could it have been so foolish? How could it have darted over the side without even thinking? Why did it run from him who was trying to save it?

You are the same as the sheep. You flee to your own destruction.

"Yes Lord," David admits aloud as he runs, understanding. "I am like that sheep. I escape the hands that love me. I depart from your loving staff."

You will lead my people. I will be their God.
"All praise to you," David agrees.

I will put you over my house of Israel, and deliver your enemies before you until they are a footstool.

David cannot keep tears from coming. They streak down his blood-splattered face. Branches strike his head and body as he weaves through the forest like a hare.

Why? I do not deserve this, he thinks. Who am I? Who is my father?

I shall pour iron into your bones and fire into your blood, and I will do these things to make my name great among all the nations.

David basks in the presence of Yahweh, in the jaws of sadness and triumph, for Yahweh is in all of those things. He feels his toes gripping the rocks, barefoot like the beast he is pursuing, and he feels like a monster himself, a terrible monster that will slaughter the enemies of the Lord.

David emerges from the forest onto a rocky slope that leads to a peak. The view of the hill country is stunning, but David ignores this because the remaining bear is near the peak, and Speckle Leg is still in its mouth.

David climbs the hill as fast as a mountain ram, breathing hard and sweating from the effort, but, strangely, not feeling tired anymore. The fire inside of him is both power and pain, and it hurts him as it rages, push him harder and faster.

The bear senses him as it runs up the slope and stops. It turns and looks at him, the sheep looking small in its mouth.

David lets the anger flood back into him. He loves the blood, the hate, the rage, the fear, all that comes with battle. He climbs up the slope hand over hand. It would take a normal man an hour to scale that mountainside, but David is up it in mere moments.

The bear stands up on its hind legs and extends its front ones, towering and ominous, its black fur matted with mud and leaves. The stench from the animal is overwhelming.

As David approaches, the bear tosses the sheep from its mouth with a shake of its great head and roars. Speckle Leg tumbles across the rocks.

David feels the beauty of Yahweh, the song of the heavens, the glory of mighty struggle, and rushes into battle.

The bear is waiting, and David meets it.

He slings a pellet into its face. The bear shakes its head harshly, stunned, but then reaches out for David with its terrible paws. David avoids them, striking the bear with the staff.

The bear paws at him, but David avoids it and hooks the crook of the staff into the animal's jaws. He leaps to the backside of the bear, keeping the tension in the staff, until he has completely crossed back around to the front.

This causes the bear to lose its balance. Its fury leads it to lash out with less effectiveness and balance, and its bulk crashes against the rocks.

David is on top of it as soon as it falls. He wraps the staff around its throat and pulls. Somehow, Yahweh gives him strength yet again. He feels the knots of muscle in his arms twitching, feels as though his eyes will burst from the pressure of the strain.

The bear lurches to its hind legs again, raising itself to full height.

David presses his face against the fur to avoid the swipes of the paws, then winces as the bear rolls onto its back.

The weight of hundreds, no, thousands of shekels crushes David. He is certain that his ribs are about to shatter.

But his ribs hold, as does his grip, as do his muscles.

I will pour iron into your bones.

The bear rolls around, roaring.

I will give you battle all of your days, and you will praise me for it.

David adjusts his grip. He can feel the thick muscle of the bear's neck begin to give way to the power in his arms. The animal's breathing becomes harsher. It thrashes even more violently.

I will establish your throne forever, for my name is great.

David no longer feels the agony of the struggle. He is gone. He is in the quiet of the field, sunlight on his face, watching the insects fly, watching the sheep graze, feeling the comforting loneliness of the forest, humming the songs of love and devotion and war.

He screams aloud a final time and wrenches the bear's throat. The spine snaps, and the monster goes limp. There, on the field of blood, in the hills of his youth, your father began to learn of battle, my king.

He felt the anguish of loss, the triumph of standing over a dead enemy.

But the day was not over for him yet. His hardest battle was yet to come.

David is panting, exhausted. At the bear's death, the fires in his body were snuffed out, and he feels as though he has aged a hundred years, and that he is too weak to even move.

It takes David a while to crawl out from under the bear's corpse, which feels even heavier to him lifeless. He emerges from under the bloody mass of fur and bile after a long, painful struggle.

He lays on his side, panting, and looks for the sheep. Then he remembers that they have scattered throughout the forest, back into the meadow, over the hill, everywhere. He shakes his head. It would be a long afternoon herding them up again.

Speckle Leg.

David spots him nearby, staring at him stupidly. It lets out a bleat.

David lets himself laugh in relief, then looks at the sky. A brilliant blue day, a remarkable gift from Yahweh. Sweat pours from his brow. His tunic is soaked with blood. A beautiful day. Everything is a gift from Yahweh.

I will be ready, God of my people, he thinks to himself. I will always be ready, whenever you bless me with battle. Though it hurts, I will always be ready. He remembers the dead sheep at the base of the cliff.

Not now. Celebrate the victory.

He is thirsty, tired, and realizes he is hungrier than he has ever known. He picks up his staff and makes his way down the hill and to the forest path with Speckle Leg at his heel. He grabs the first two sheep he sees by the scruffy wool of their necks and leads them through the bramble to the edge of the open field. They bleat as he pulls them.

In the clearing, he raises his fingers to his mouth to whistle. It is the peculiar call that all shepherds give to their sheep, and that their sheep recognize. Not all of them obey him when he summons. There are some stragglers. But most of them run wildly in his direction, bleating from fear.

They are shaking as they draw near, the fear of the predators still covering them. He reaches out and pats their necks one by one.

Your father, oh king, told me once that the covering never left him all of his days, but there were times, especially following a battle, that he felt a crushing weight. A depression that resonated deep in his soul, and he had to cry out to Yahweh for relief.

He never understood it. Even as an old man, he told me about long periods after great victories where he wished to die. That Yahweh would come and take his life and be done with it. Why have such triumphs, only to be followed by the pit of darkness?

Your father was a man of contradictions in many ways. I have never seen one so in love with Yahweh, and yet I have also never seen one suffer so desperately for reasons known only to himself.

There were the rebellions of your brothers, the scheming of those in his own ranks of warriors, the bickering and maneuvering of his wives and concubines, the endless pressures of ruling a fractured kingdom of tribes, the ever-present specter of our enemies from every side. These were all understandable reasons to be vexed. You know of them yourself, after all, and you handle it with grace, if I may say so, your majesty.

And yet it does not seem that these things were the cause of his agony. He was a man of passions. A man of highest heights and deepest pits. A man firm like the stones of Carmel, yet soft as the lambs he once watched over. Then, perhaps, the suffering in his soul was caused by the Adversary. The enemies of Yahweh, the shadowy ones you have heard your father and Benaiah and the rest speak of, who appeared and contended with them on occasion, and did not behave as mere men.

This was your father's first day of war. He would come to know power and might...and he would come to know loss and sorrow. They would both affect him all of his days.

Nevertheless, we must continue.

David climbs down from the high country with his sheep. He has a hard time keeping his footing on the rocks, for he is exhausted from the battle. As he walks, he hums his song of deliverance and victory.

But, slowly, the dread creeps into his spirit. It is the first time he has experienced the let-down of battle, the loss of desire to live that comes upon all warriors and does not distinguish between victors and vanquished.

His feet become heavy. His vision clouds with darkness. He is suddenly angry and depressed and euphoric, all at the same time. He loves killing. Cannot wait to kill again. He hates killing. Then he loves it again.

The sheep wander out from the path, a few trot towards the

forest again, and he is furious.

"Did I not just save you? Do you want to be eaten? Then be eaten!"

He stumbles down the hillside, ignoring the sheep. The sheep's bloody body at the base of the cliff appears in his vision, mangled and torn. Lifeless. Lifeless as he felt now, and he swats at the air to try to drive the vision away.

Bright red blood on the fleece. The mark of his failure to save the sheep named Cedar. His failure in all things.

"Lord, what is victory?" he cries out.

There is no answer in the stillness. Insects chirp, birds call, all is pure around him.

The beasts are gone, and yet he feels them still.

David eventually drives the sheep into the corrals for the night. His father's home is on the outskirts of Bethlehem. In those days it was a sleepy town, my king, a small outpost in the hill country paid attention to by no one.

It is evening by the time he stands at the entry to his father's house. Jesse of Bethlehem had flocks and many sons, and was respected among the people of the town. There were always people coming and going to conduct business with him. It is a lively home, and yet David never feels comfortable inside of it.

Inside, David can hear the laughter of Eliab, the firstborn, the center of everyone's life, it seems. David does not hate his older brother, and he had never truly felt hated in return, but the day the prophet visited with the oil had changed that.

Now David is the scourge of the family. There is no pride in him from his brothers, only resentment and envy.

His older sister Zeruiah, with her sons Joab, Abishai, and Asahel were visiting. The family was large, and happy much of the time. Except when he was there.

You must pardon my intrusion again, lord, but I have often wondered about those days. What it must have been like seeing your father and his nephew Joab together as youths. Though Zeruiah's sons were his nephews, they were contemporaries in age. Was there tension between them? Your father never told me, although it seems as though they got along well. Perhaps it is the events that followed when they were older men that distorts the truth of their relationship in those early times.

Joab was loyal to your father, no question. You sent Benaiah to do what he needed to do and remove the threat to your throne, and Joab had spilled much innocent blood, but I wonder at it.

David stands outside of the doorway, girds up his courage, and enters.

There is a grand meal spread out on the rug. All of his six brothers are there, as well as his two sisters and their children.

David's brother Eliab looks up from the food and conversation. His face falls when he sees David's appearance. There is blood, torn clothing, and animal fur all over him.

"What happened?"

Everyone stops talking and turns to David.

David swallows, his courage deserting him. "I battled with lions and bears."

They stare at him. Eliab seems taken aback, but then his eyes turn hard and he rises angrily.

"Is it not enough that you are to be our ruler one day, now you must go out and pretend to kill fearsome creatures by yourself?"

David averts his eyes. He tries to speak again, but his words are slow. His father is somewhere in the room. He tries to spot him.

The old man is watching him from a corner near a lamp. Everyone turns to look at him, awaiting his response.

"Did you lose any of the sheep?"

David looks around the room. They are all staring at him. Unloving. Uncaring. His brothers surely plotting his demise. His father weary of him.

And though he has shown great courage all through the

day, though he has done the unthinkable and killed the great predators with only his staff and his sling and the strength of his arms, he loses courage in that room.

"I...lost one."

Jesse shakes his head and looks away. Eliab begins to pronounce things against David, his brothers agree, the women and girls of his family whisper to one another, and David feels shame wash over him like a spring flood.

They do not care for his story or his reasons. They only want to condemn him.

David is starving and the smell of the food drives him to the brink of madness, but he turns and leaves.

————————

Outside, in the growing darkness, David sees a figure. It is familiar to him. The man from under the tree earlier that afternoon.

David's mood has soured such that he says, "Where were you today? I needed help. I lost a sheep."

"I was there."

"I did not see you."

"Yes you did."

David remembers the vision now, the heavenly armies above him.

"Why do you think the bear stopped at the top of the mountain? Why did the lion run for the drop-off where you would be able to catch him?" the warrior asks.

David thinks about it for a moment. Then says, "But I still had to fight them."

The warrior looks at David as though the statement amused him. "You will never be spared from battle, young king. Battle is what the Lord of Heaven and Earth has forged you for. He has merely promised you victories."

David looks down at the rocks at his feet, considering the words. Then he looks back up to ask another question.

The warrior is gone.

David finds Speckle Leg by the stone fence on the boundary of his father's land. He pats the sheep on its head, checks the bandage on its neck, and then it follows him into the woods as he climbs a small knoll that affords a view of the valley around him. The sun is nearly gone.

After a while, his shame leaves. He is alone, as it ought to be. He tells himself that he no longer cares what they are saying in his father's house. He does not need his father's approval or the approval of his brothers. Only Yahweh. But in the quiet, now that he is alone, how he craves the day when Jesse will gaze upon him approvingly.

David listens to the breeze in the treetops. The air grows colder. The sheep next to him nuzzles for grass between the rocks.

"I felt him today, Speckle Leg. I felt Yahweh. I felt his power deliver us. I wonder how..." He watches the stars twinkle in the deep purple heavens. A purple no man can dye. Only the handiwork of Yahweh.

He looks down at his arms, scarred from battle. Thinks of the impossible strength in them when he needed it most. The pain in his heart for the lost sheep is still there, but David feels... soothed. Warmed. Comforted. As though despite the agony and darkness of grief, he will pass through it like how a shadow flees before dawn.

"I think I will call it... the covering."

———————————

No one has heard this story, my lord.

As you might suppose, it is simply too hard to believe, even for many who revered the great king, though your father mentioned it to King Saul when he was a young man and the giant from Gath taunted Israel's armies in the Elah. Many think the defeat of the Philistines that day was his greatest victory. Perhaps it is so.

But in the opinion of your humble servant, and for the purpose of this writing, the battle in the fields and forests of the sheep country resonated in our kingdom the longest.

It was there your father met the power of Yahweh. He had known of it, to be sure. He remembered the day the prophet Samuel poured the anointing oil over his head. But to know of something, and then to truly know something...well, those are different. He knew about the covering before that day. Afterwards, he knew the covering.

It was a victory in a desolate, lonely place between only David and the Lord. There were no crowds to cheer, no women to trill and sing songs, no old men to tell the story to the young men around a campfire. Only Yahweh as an audience, and that was enough. As Eleazar always said, if courage holds in the small battles, it will hold in the great ones.

I am told that your grandfather Jesse was a noble man. But I fear he did not know the special nature of your father. Your father suffered for it. Even late in life, surrounded by the crowds of grateful admirers, he was the loneliest person I ever knew. No one can understand the burden of the kingdom but the king himself.

As an old man, dying in his bed while telling me this tale, the passion of youth emerged from David's soul again.

When the story was complete, the king looked at me directly in the eyes. A strange gesture, as you know, for the king to look so intently at a mere servant. He was nearly blind by then, so I do not know if he could see me, but his eyes were fiery like those of a young man, their amber and honey color raging for an instant.

"I do not care how you portray me, for I have been a wicked man," he said. "But you will make much of the Lord. You will tell the people that he was the great victor in every winning battle of my life. Ensure that my son knows these things, and that the knowledge girds him like a man."

And so you have this tale, my lord.

David, son of Jesse, king over Israel and vanquisher of the enemies of Yahweh, was a mere man. A more difficult person to understand will never be known. He failed many times. But he never turned aside from the Lord to idols or other gods, and in the darkness of his soul during his worst hours, he always came back with a broken and contrite spirit before Yahweh, the Lord of Hosts.

Perhaps that is why the Lord never abandoned him. Perhaps that is why we loved him.

PATRIOT *academy*

sponsored by wallbuilders and the torch of freedom foundation
{ raising up a new generation to **LEAD THE CHANGE** }

CHALLENGE YOUR IDEA OF GOVERNMENT

At Patriot Academy, you don't just learn about government, you live it. This summer, you and your fellow students, ages 16-25, will take over the Texas state government at the Capitol Building in Austin, Texas. You will work together to form a fully functioning mock government, drafting legislation, running committee meetings, debating bills, electing leaders and passing laws.

CONFRONT THE ISSUES OF TODAY

In a fast-paced, interactive format, elected officials and experts will explain today's most relevant issues. Through media relations training, public speaking workshops and spirited debate, you will learn to articulate what you believe and why. Patriot Academy will equip you to effect change for the issues that matter most to you, whether as a concerned citizen or political candidate.

CHAMPION THE CAUSE OF FREEDOM

If you want to be a part of a new generation of young leaders poised to change the future of American politics, join us at Patriot Academy. You won't want to miss it!

FOR MORE INFORMATION OR TO APPLY, VISIT US AT
WWW.PATRIOTACADEMY.COM

BRING
Wallbuilder's LIVE *host,*
RICK GREEN's

Constitution Alive!

to YOUR area

*H*istory and government do NOT have to be boring! Rick Green brings the Constitution and citizenship to life through compelling, entertaining, and even funny stories about the lives, fortunes, and sacred honor sacrificed to make America the most powerful, most free nation in the history of the world.

> "I have never heard a more down-to-earth, common sense version of our Constitution and what it was intended to do than the one given by Rick Green." -Joni C., TX

> "Having Rick speak to us about our nation's history was truly a blessing. Not only did he impart historical facts, he gave us direction and motivation to stay in the battle for our country." -Lyleann T., TX

> "We have been looking for a class just like this for years! It is concise, engaging, interesting, and ties in our Biblical foundations. Just the right balance of studying the actual text, historical context and current events." -Lori G., WA

> "The seminar was gripping, informative, and impacting! It was so great to be properly informed on what our nation was really founded on and our rights as citizens of the U.S. Each person who attended left with a lasting impression and gained fresh insight about our nation. The Constitution Seminar was a great tool for our church and we are excited to see the fruit that comes from each person who attended." -Pastor Mark

*S*chedule your class now and let's help restore America back to her Founding Principles!

One of the most dynamic & inspirational speakers in America today, nationally known Constitutional teacher, and co-host of the national radio program "WallBuilders Live!" with David Barton, heard on more than 200 stations across America:

"Inspiring and equipping citizens to preserve liberty"

As a community leader, you have the unique opportunity to host a live Constitution class with Rick Green where you will be providing an environment for attendees to regain the working knowledge every citizen once had of our Constitution.

Rick will take you back to the events of 1776 and the Declaration of Independence onto 1787 and the Constitutional Convention, and step by step through the Constitutional Amendments, right up to the current debates in our nation today covering topics such as nullification, impeachment, the Electoral College vs. National Popular Vote, First Amendment Freedom of Religion, individual God-given rights. vs. group government-given rights. is the Constitution a living document, and much more.

Schedule your class now and let's help restore America back to her Founding Principles!

www.RickGreen.com
512.858.4825

"The Constitutional Class presented by Rick Green was a great experience for our church as well as many members throughout the Portland metro area. Rick was instructional, practical, funny, and very entertaining as he presented a clear explanation of how the founding fathers view our Constitution. I would recommend any church hosting such a class and also having Rick stay over to speak to their Sunday morning crowd. We had a great weekend, and we were enriched and blessed. Thanks, Rick!" -Pastor Mike, Beavercreek, OR

{ "Every member of the State ought diligently to read and study the Constitution of his country... By knowing their rights, they will sooner perceive when they are violated and be the better prepared to defend and assert them."
- Chief Justice John Jay }

• also available as a webinar session or DVD recording •

THE LEADER'S EDGE

POWER *of* PURPOSEFUL COMMUNICATION

THE LEADER'S EDGE

Living YOUR PURPOSE

Using the proven strategies of the most successful people on the planet, the interactive Living YOUR Purpose helps you create a detailed blueprint for building your dreams; a step by step road map for fulfilling your purpose; and a clear, easy-to-follow track to run on, in order to reach your destination... down to the details of your daily tasks connected to each of your specific goals that are part of living your purpose and passion.

What gives you joy and pleasure and a sense of purpose?

"I am so excited to tell you about the powerful tool that I've used in my life for the last 20 years in planning my goals, identifying my life purpose, and staying on track to accomplish my mission.

In **Living Your Purpose**, I will help you walk through the steps to identify what's most important to you in life and what you need to get it. I'm even more excited that now you can track your goals, get daily life lessons, and so much more through **Living Your Purpose**.

Join me on this journey of discovering your purpose and living it!"

"So often life feels like an impossible 5000 piece puzzle. LYP helped guide me by asking the right questions to find God's purpose for my life." – **BRADY**

"The LYP program radically changed my life. It gave me the tools to identify and pursue my purpose and calling. I recommend the program for anyone who wants to get their priorities in order and start moving toward a more fulfilling and successful life." – **KYLE**

MORE INFO @
www.RickGreen.com

entrepreneur   nurse   pastor   mother   coach   lawyer   athlete   congressman

W O R L D ◇ C H A N G E R S

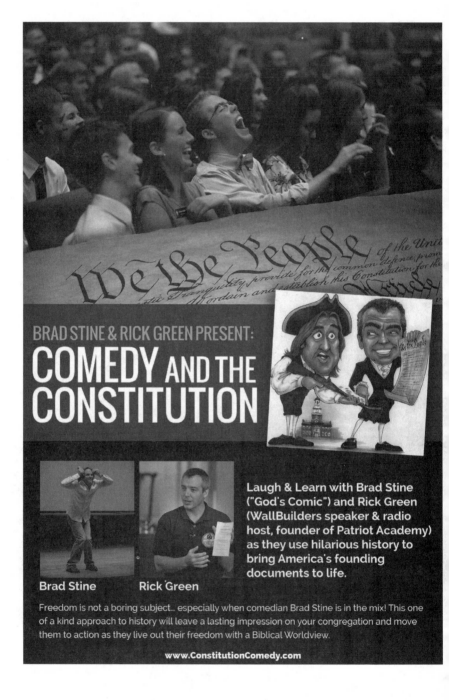

BRAD STINE & RICK GREEN PRESENT:

COMEDY AND THE CONSTITUTION

Brad Stine   Rick Green

Laugh & Learn with Brad Stine ("God's Comic") and Rick Green (WallBuilders speaker & radio host, founder of Patriot Academy) as they use hilarious history to bring America's founding documents to life.

Freedom is not a boring subject... especially when comedian Brad Stine is in the mix! This one of a kind approach to history will leave a lasting impression on your congregation and move them to action as they live out their freedom with a Biblical Worldview.

www.ConstitutionComedy.com

Get the full 12 Hour Constitution Alive Class Package!

The entire Constitution Class recorded in the very cradle of liberty, Independence Hall in Philadelphia, as well as all the additional sessions with David Barton in the amazing WallBuilders Library, on 4 DVD's, as well as an MP3 Audio CD of the entire course. These discs include Q&A from attendees and teaching from Rick's four children.

Also includes David Barton's CD sharing how the Founding Fathers pointed out specific parts of the Constitution that establish its generally religious and explicitly Christian nature.

Order today at **WallBuilders.com** for your family library or as a gift for others. Use it to teach this Constitution Class in your Sunday School, your home, or at a local Tea Party. If you would like to use the DVD's to teach the class, bulk pricing on this workbook is available.